CONFEDERATE CENTENNIAL STUDIES

WM. STANLEY HOOLE, *Editor-in-Chief*

Number *Thirteen*

LINCOLN'S PLAN OF RECONSTRUCTION

By

WILLIAM B. HESSELTINE

Lincoln's Plan of Reconstruction

By

WILLIAM B. HESSELTINE

GLOUCESTER, MASS.

PETER SMITH

1963

27480

Contents

Preface

ANDREW JOHNSON, Lincoln's successor in the White House, upon whose shoulders the burdens and the contentions of the "Reconstruction Period" fell, liked to allege that he was carrying out Lincoln's plans for the reconstruction of the South after the Civil War. Commentators then and later have accepted Johnson's contention, and many of them have engaged in futile speculations about how different things would have been, if Lincoln had lived to complete his second term. His plan, rather than the plan of Congress, would then—perhaps—have been put into operation and would have saved the nation from the dozen years of turmoil that followed the surrender of the Confederate forces.

In this monograph, originally prepared as a series of lectures at Memphis State University, I have attempted to examine the basis for this contention; to survey the various plans that Lincoln instituted, operated, and abandoned; and to look at the evolution of the rival program of the Radical Republicans in Congress. Implicit in the story is the construction of the American nation from the ruins of the old Federal Union.

University of Wisconsin   WILLIAM B. HESSELTINE
Fall, 1959

LINCOLN'S PLAN OF RECONSTRUCTION

CHAPTER I

The Border States

No LEGEND of the Civil War is more persistent than the belief that, if Lincoln had lived, the years of reconstruction that followed would have been different: that the magnanimous Lincoln, the great humanitarian, would not only have restored the "proper practical relations" between the Southern states and the Federal government, but also would have effected an emotional reconciliation between the members of the momentarily estranged American family. The legend rests in part upon wishful thinking, in part upon a realization that Lincoln's policy was pragmatic and realistic and relatively unaffected by the epidemic of hate-psychosis that paralyzed the reasoning powers of many national leaders of the Northern Republican party. Perhaps, in the first months after Appomattox the Southern people wanted most to have their sins forgiven, to be welcomed back into the arms of the family and be acknowledged as equals in settling the difficulties that had divided them. Disappointed in this hope, they gave credence to the father-image of a Lincoln who, if only he had lived, would have forgiven the prodigals and set out a feast, complete with fatted calf, to celebrate their return.

Reconstruction might indeed have been different had Lincoln lived, and reconciliation might conceivably have come quicker and more completely, but any speculation about the probable course that it would have taken must rest upon an appraisal of Lincoln's policy and of the direction in which reconstruction was already going, when insane John Wilkes Booth's bullet brought new actors upon the scene. The

processes of reconstruction were already far advanced
when, a few hours after Lincoln's death, Generals William
Tecumseh Sherman and Joseph Eggleston Johnston met in
North Carolina and agreed upon terms that would end the
war. Reconstruction had long been uppermost in the minds
of Northern leaders, Republicans and Democrats, social
reformers and economic planners, practical politicians and
tinkering theorists alike.

Reconstruction was, in fact, the basic issue of the Civil
War. The desire to re-make the South, to reorganize its
social system, to bring its divergent economy into the main
stream of American life, to impose peculiar concepts of
government and of constitutional interpretation upon the
Southern states had been the reason for beginning the war
and for prosecuting it with vigor, despite tremendous losses
in human life and costs in national wealth. In the fullest
sense, secession was the South's effort to avoid the reconstruction which Southern political astrologers foresaw in
the rising star of Republican control of the Federal government. Mississippi's convention carefully pointed to the
prospect that "in pursuance of their hostility to us" they
had determined that "the powers of this Government are
to be used for the dishonor and overthrow of the Southern
section of this great Confederacy."   South Carolina, whose
politicians had long surveyed the skies and found omens in
the adverse conjunctions, hysterically pointed out that "the
guarantees of the Constitution will then no longer exist"
after Lincoln's inauguration. "The equal rights of the states
will be lost. The Slave-holding states will no longer have
the power of self government, or self protection, and the
Federal Government will have become their enemy. Sectional
interest and animosity will deepen the irritation; and all
hope of remedy is rendered vain, by the fact that the public
opinion at the North has invested a great political error
with the sanctions of a more erroneous religious belief."[1]

---

[1] Mississippi *Laws*, 1860 (Jackson, 1860), 43ff.; "South Carolina
Declaration of Causes of Secession," in Frank Moore (ed.), *Rebellion
Record . . .* (New York, 1864-1867), I, 3ff.

Essentially, the various compromise proposals proposed to recognize and establish a duality in the American government—to reconstruct both the constitution and the thought-patterns of the American people by provisions for guaranteeing an autonomous position for the South. President James Buchanan, submitting his distracted message of December, 1860, proposed calling a constitutional convention which would formally recognize slavery in the states that wanted it, and in the common territories. Congressmen paid no attention to the suggestion and proceeded to discuss compromise proposals within the two houses. Perhaps, indeed, a convention would have contained no abler men than were present in the House and Senate, but it might have assembled them in a single body under a popular mandate to reconstruct the Union and without the immediate necessity of weighing each proposition in a partisan balance. As it was, the struggle for political advantage permeated the discussion and led to the rejection of each device to establish a dual system. The propositions before them, responsible and irresponsible, varied from the subtile to the overt, but duality characterized each of them. Least concerned with duality was the ingenious proposition of Minnesota's Senator Henry M. Rice to add parts of the national domain to the adjacent states of Minnesota, Oregon, and California, and divide the remainder into two states to be simultaneously admitted to the Union. This would have effectively disposed of the "territorial" question which, at least on the surface, was the issue dividing the country. Rice contended that his device would maintain the political balance indefinitely. No one gave serious attention to his scheme, but Ohio's Congressman John Sherman came near to imitating it, when he proposed dividing all territory into states and admitting them immediately. This would have fixed the status of slavery in the South and would have avoided all further controversies. At the other extreme of duality were the proposals of Georgia's Robert Toombs, Virginia's R. M. T. Hunter, and Tennessee's Andrew Johnson. Toombs proposed guaranteeing property in slaves and giving slaveholding states a veto over all laws which would modify the guarantees. Hunter carried the concept of duality further by reviving John C. Calhoun's plan for a dual executive. Each section should elect a president, one to serve four years and be succeeded by each other, each should approve all treaties in addition to two thirds of the Senate, and each law should have the approval of both, though the veto of either could be overridden by a majority of the senators from his section. The Supreme Court would have five justices from the slave states and five from the free. Still more drastic was Andrew Johnson, whose proposed duality added the unique feature of democratic elections. The Tennessean favored the direct election of senators, the division of the country into electoral districts for presidential elections, and a run-off election between the two highest candidates, if there was no majority. He would also have the president and the vice-president alternately come from the North and the South, have the Supreme Court divided into three classes, each serving four years, and each equally divided between the free and the slave states. This was a proposal for drastic reconstruction rather than a compromise of the controversial issues of the moment.

Yet, even though Johnson's, Hunter's and Toombs's proposals received scant notice, they contained the same element as the propositions that received major attention. These were the compromises offered by Kentucky's John J. Crittenden in the Senate and the propositions that emerged from the debates of the Washington Peace Conference. Both proposed dividing the territories between slavery and freedom, and giving guarantees to the South that the arrangement would be permanent.[2]

Emerging from the discussions over compromise, both in and out of Congress, were several approaches to the problems of reconstruction. One was the attitude of the voices of the business community which favored any settlement

[2] Allan Nevins, *The Emergence of Lincoln* (New York, 1952), II, 385-440.

short of war. Some spokesmen of business favored the
Crittenden Compromise, some favored letting the "erring
sisters" of the South "depart in peace." On December 29,
1860 Amos Lawrence could write Crittenden that everyone
was watching his efforts at pacification and that "nine out
of ten of our people would laugh at anyone who would tell
them that blood must be shed." Others could suggest to
Crittenden that Kentucky, New Jersey, and the other central
states form a new government with the Southerners in it,
and "leaving all the New England States out, to burn
witches and Quakers and affiliate with Niggers. After we
get rid of them we shall have peace."[3] No responsible
spokesman of finance or industry spoke out for coercion or
expressed an idea that war or subsequent reconstruction
would benefit the business community.

On the other hand, the discussions brought out vigorous
opposition to compromises from men who favored a social
reconstruction of the South. For long years the Abolitionists had agitated against the "sin" of slavery, and in time
politicians seeking to make a solid North had taken up their
indignant moral crusade against the peculiar institution and
used it to consolidate their sectional position. Now, in the
secession crisis the social reformers took an intransigent
position. "No union with slaveholders" had been an ancient
demand. As the slaveholders departed from the Union,
Charles Sumner steadily voted against all compromises with
slavery. When Charles Francis Adams, son of John Quincy
Adams, who had done as much as any man to focus Northern
attention on the political aspects of Abolitionism, voted to
organize New Mexico Territory with the slavery question
left to the decision of the inhabitants, Sumner ceased all
social intercourse with him. "Let the slave powers extort
from our fears one sacrifice of the principles on which we
fought," he told Abolitionist John Jay, "and our humiliation
will be complete." From the beginning Sumner preferred
war to compromise and demanded that the war end slavery

[3] In John J. Crittenden Papers, Library of Congress (hereinafter
JJCP).

and force a social reconstruction upon the South. Like
Sumner, others who shared the trustee tradition in America
—believing themselves specially elect as stewards of the
Lord to reorder and regulate society for the greater glory
of God—rejected the Southern proposals for duality and
looked forward to war as a means of reorganizing society.
Even though some peace societies passed resolutions asserting that any concession was preferable to civil war and
national ruin, pacifist leaders made a compromise with
their principles and endorsed an unyielding stand against
the Secessionists. Amasa Walker, long an active pacifist
leader, was more deeply incensed against slavery than he was
against war, and he rationalized his apostasy by the conven-
ient theory that the coming civil war was only the proper
maintenance of law and order by the properly constituted
authorities. He too looked forward to social reconstruction.

But the primary consideration in the rejection of reconstruction through compromise was the interests of the
newly victorious Republican party. Douglas Democrats
and Bell and Everett Constitutional Union men favored
compromise. "All history and the lives of all persons,"
declared the Detroit *Free Press,* December 27, 1860, "are
made up of concessions and compromises." But "Mr. Lincoln and his party" would "yield nothing, concede nothing,
compromise nothing. And so the Union must go on to
destruction." It was, stated the Albany *Argus,* December
15, only justice to give the South equality in the territories.
The Republicans in Congress could give "instant and permanent peace" to the country, "and become saviors instead
of destroyers of the nation." But Horace Greeley replied
in the New York *Tribune,* December 2 and 31, that the South
demanded "a naked and absolute surrender of our cherished
principles." The editor trusted that Crittenden's compromise would not be adopted "by the aid of Republican votes."
Any compromise, bluntly warned papers in Minnesota,
would undermine the future of the Republican party.[4]

[4] See Roman J. Zorn, "Minnesota Public Opinion and the Secession
Controversy, December, 1860-April, 1861," *Mississippi Valley Historical Review,* XXXVI, 445 (Dec., 1949).

The key to Republican policy in those days of crisis was President-elect Abraham Lincoln. In many ways his position as the nominal head of the Republican party was anomalous. He had not been the outstanding candidate of the party before his nomination at Chicago, and he had contributed little during the campaign to his election. Whatever power the party had was in the states and their leaders, especially the governors, had nominated and elected him. With only two exceptions, the states whose electoral votes went to the Republican gubernatorial candidates had won election by greater majorities than had Lincoln. But it was Lincoln who was assuming control of the Federal government. The governors sought to advise him and to guide his conduct, but their council was divided and it remained for him to select from among them. Yet Lincoln was hardly a free agent, capable of looking at the problem before the nation with disinterested and objective statesmanship. He had not only worked to build up the Republican party, but had also carefully defined the single issue upon which all Republicans were united—opposition to the extension of slavery into the territories. "If our sense of duty forbids it," he had told a Cooper Union audience in February, 1860, "then let us stand by our duty fearlessly." There should be no yielding by Unionists to Disunionists, no deviation by "sophistical contrivances," no "reversing the divine rule and calling, not the sinners but the righteous to repentance."[5] Now, after busy months that seemed as many years later, he stood fast by his own admonitions. "Let there be no compromise on the question of extending slavery," he told Lyman Trumbull in December. "If there be, all our labor is lost, and ere long, must be done again." The dangerous ground was Popular Sovereignty: "Have none of it. Stand firm. The tug has to come, and better now than any time later." The next day he gave the same instructions to Congressman William Kellogg—if Republicans yielded, "they have us under again." "Prevent any of our friends,"

[5] Roy P. Basler (ed.), *Collected Works of Abraham Lincoln* (New Brunswick, 1953), IV, 38-39.

he told E. B. Washburne, "from demoralizing themselves."
In February, after months of discussion and as a half
dozen states were out of the Union, he told Senator William
H. Seward, "I am inflexible." Compromise would, he
reiterated, lose everything the Republicans gained by the
election.[6]

In Washington, before his inauguration, Lincoln cautiously called upon the Peace Conference, which had been
called by Virginia and which some of the more intransigent
and Secessionist states had boycotted, but he gave the delegates no hopes that he would accept any reconstruction of
the Union on the principle of duality with an autonomous
South with special guarantee for its institutions. His inaugural address appealed to the sentiment of unity but
yielded no point at issue between the sections. Clearly
Lincoln would brook no concession on the central principles
of the Republican party, and with his inauguration all talk
of compromise came to an end. Clearly, too, Lincoln's
approach to a reorganization of the nation was political.

Lincoln obviously counted heavily upon Unionist sentiment in the South. He and the men about him heard
constantly of the "false guides" who had led the Southern
people astray. "A large majority of the people of North
Alabama would today be in favor of a reunion," a Hunts-
ville resident told Andrew Johnson, "if we of the South
could only get constitutional safeguards for our Negro rights
and property." It was, a Louisville railroad man told
Lincoln, "madcaps and self-aggrandizing hotspurs" who had
deceived the "unaspiring people of the South." But throughout the reports from the South there ran one note of
warning—coercion must be avoided. "From the tone of
your papers," a South Carolinian wrote Lincoln, "one would
suppose you are relying on powder and shot to save the
union. If that is your notion, do not deceive yourself.
Powder and shot and federal troops will never save this

[6] Lincoln to Lyman Trumbull, Dec. 10, to William Kellogg, Dec. 11,
to E. B. Washburne, Dec. 13, 1860, to William H. Seward, Feb. 1, 1861
(*ibid.*, IV, 149-151, 183).

government." And from Nashville Neil S. Brown warned
Johnson that a collision would ruin Unionist sentiment in
Tennessee. "The longer force can be kept out of the South
the better." J. F. White in Chickamauga reported that the
"mulish stubbornness" of Black Republicans was crushing
out the Union spirit. Only the shedding of blood would
"alienate the common people." But if collision came, "then
all hope of reconstruction is at an end, the Southern Confederacy though borne down and perhaps defeated will find
a place in the annals of history—and a lodgement in the
affection of its deluded subjects which at present it does not
possess." There was Unionism in the South, but Lincoln
failed to take direction from the advice of Union men.[7]

In the course of the war which followed, Abraham Lincoln slowly and pragmatically evolved his own plan of
reconstruction. His program, like that of other Northerners
who rejected compromise in the winter of 1860-61, was
committed to unity, and had no place for a dual system with
special officers to protect the South or special guarantees
for Southern peculiar institutions. But other Northerners
were committed to social reconstruction, and in the course
of the war new economic groups, developing out of the
conflict, emerged with plans for economic reconstruction
of the nation. Lincoln, however, endorsed neither economic
interests nor social philosophy—nor did he become the
victim of war-engendered hysteria. His program remained
political, with the interests of the Republican party uppermost in his thoughts.

The first steps in the development of Lincoln's plan for
reconstruction came in the states of the Upper South and
evolved into what was, somewhat incoherently, known as his
Border State policy. He began with politics, and in the
manner of a politician he tried by political devices to prevent a further breach of the Union. In his thinking, as
became explicit in his first message to Congress in June,

[7] Joseph C. Bradley to Andrew Johnson, March 8, 1861 (Andrew
Johnson Papers, Library of Congress, hereinafter AJP); Norwin
Green to Lincoln, March 14, 1861 (Robert Todd Lincoln Papers,
Library of Congress, hereinafter RTLP).

secession was political. The masses of the Southern people
were loyal at heart to the Union, but they had been misled
by their political leaders. All they needed to return to their
loyalty were new and loyal leaders whom they could follow.
For all of his talk of principle and duty, Lincoln gave no
thought to the concept that principle and duty might actuate
the South's leaders and people. Accordingly, in the month
following his accession, besieged on every hand by fawning
office-seekers of his own party, he tried to find suitable
leaders for the misguided Southerners and to reward them
with offices. He found places in his cabinet for Missouri's
Edward Bates and Maryland's Montgomery Blair, who also
had Missouri connections, but he ignored the insistent
clamor of erratic Cassius M. Clay of Kentucky, who had
long battled against the slavocracy of the Blue Grass State
and had proved himself unable to lead Kentuckians to
abolitionism or the Republicans.[8] He sought the support
of John A. Gilmer of North Carolina, who failed to respond
to his overtures. In general, the President sought the
support of Old Whigs and Constitutional Unionists, hoping
to bind them to the Republican party by patronage. He
settled patronage squabbles in Maryland by dividing post-
masterships, customhouse offices, and foreign consulates
between Montgomery Blair and Constitutional Unionist
Henry Winter Davis, and gave more support in Delaware
to the slate of office-seekers prepared by a Constitutional
Unionist than to that offered by the little state's diligent
Republican organizer. But his actions met opposition which
presaged future conflicts. "I would be recreant to party
duty," W. G. Snethen informed Lincoln, "if I didn't tell you
of the alarm of Republicans of Baltimore . . . at the
common rumor that some of the federal offices are to be
given to Bell men." If it were true, he added, it would "be
fatal to the golden opportunity now afforded of our gaining
Republican ascendancy in Maryland." In western Virginia,
the removal of Union sympathizers in Wheeling and

[8] Harry J. Carman and Reinhard H. Luthin, *Lincoln and the Patronage* (New York, 1943), 18-19.

Parkersburg brought additional protests and arguments that this would ruin the Union party.[9] He sent Cassius M. Clay to Russia, perhaps as much to exile as to reward him, and distributed minor patronage plums to old friends and Unionists.

In those states where Lincoln could find Unionists to accept office, he created a nucleus of Republican support. It was scarcely enough by itself to prevent secession, but it contributed to the states' remaining, by a narrow margin, in the Union. His policy was politically successful. Virginia, Tennessee, North Carolina, and Arkansas, where Lincoln either failed to find or to look for Unionist leaders, seceded. Maryland, Missouri, and Kentucky, with varying degrees of discomfort, remained in the Union.

Two weeks before Sumter, Lincoln received from S. A. Hurlbut a totally misleading estimate of the situation of the Border States. Hurlbut had gone to Charleston with Lincoln's bodyguard, Ward Hill Lamon, who completely deceived the Charlestonians about Lincoln's purposes. Hurlbut had abandoned Lamon, but he in turn was deceived by his hosts. From South Carolina leaders Hurlbut got the idea that Southern rulers did not relish the thought of having the Border States in the Confederacy. The Constitution of the Confederate States, he explained, was designed to perpetuate the rule of the upper classes and had nothing in it for the people. But the proportion of white men in the states of the Upper South was too great, and the Southern leaders only wanted eastern North Carolina and eastern Virginia in the Confederacy. Yet, out of this estimate Hurlbut drew the conclusion that the seven states already seceded were irretrievably gone. If Lincoln enforced the laws there would be war—and, if the North successfully prosecuted the war, "the United States can do nothing better than to receive them back into our national family, an angry, sullen, disgraced, and dangerous people." Whatever may have been Lincoln's hope that the Border States would be unwelcome in the South, he did not accept

[9] W. G. Snethen to Lincoln, March 25, 1861 (RTLP).

the conclusion that the Lower South was irretrievably gone. More in keeping with his action was the advice he got from his fellow Illinoisian, Orville H. Browning, who was sure that delay was crushing out "a large party in the slave states." It was better, he advised, to defend the Union at the point of a bayonet and maintain by force the supremacy of the Constitution and the laws.[10]

After Sumter, the call for troops, and the secession of the Upper South, Lincoln quickly found a situation that revealed that neither patronage nor the "mystic chords of memory," to which he had appealed in his inaugural, were sufficient to insure adhesion to the Union or to build a political party. Within the next few months in Maryland, Missouri, and Kentucky, Lincoln added other ingredients to that which would become his plan of reconstruction.

Maryland's adherence to the Union, by whatever means necessary, was essential to the continuance of the government. Fortunately, Maryland's Governor Thomas D. Hicks was a Constitutional Unionist who had resisted and delayed the moves of his state's Secessionist element to call the legislature to consider Maryland's relations to the Union. The legislature, however, would meet within a few weeks of the time that the first troops came rushing to the "defense" of the Federal capital. Rioters met the first contingent of Massachusetts troops, and blood flecked the streets of Baltimore. The city's mayor and Governor Hicks took steps to prevent more troops marching through the excited city, and for a week, with railroad bridges burned and telegraph wires down, Washington was effectively out of communication with the North. Then, General Benjamin F. Butler, who would make many more contributions to the techniques of reconstruction, leading a larger body of Massachusetts troops which had come by sea, "captured" Annapolis and the United States Academy, occupied Baltimore, repaired wires and bridges, and restored communications. For his pains Butler received a reprimand, but

[10] S. A. Hurlbut and Orville H. Browning to Lincoln, March 25, 26, 1861 (RTLP).

his drastic settlement remained in force. The military police Baltimore, and Lincoln ordered General Winfield Scott to proclaim martial law and suspend the writ of *habeas corpus*. Soon, with Lincoln's approval, the military arrested known Secessionist members of the legislature— thus assuring a Unionist majority which would not call a convention. Maryland, a Confederate soldier reported to Tennessee's Governor Isham G. Harris, "is terribly oppressed. She is without arms and half Republican. The enemy search their houses for arms, and practically force the 'sedition law' of olden time. They have their legislature, at Fred'k, surrounded by Republican soldiers and are about to muzzle the press."[11] In fact, Maryland was an occupied region. Substantially, it was the first Southern state to be conquered, and the first to be reconstructed. Under the protection of Federal bayonets, Henry Winter Davis and Montgomery Blair could organize and marshall their antagonistic factions of the Republican party.

Simultaneous with the conquest and the occupation of Maryland were the events in Missouri, and here within a few months new elements were added to the developing program of reconstruction. Unlike Maryland's Hicks, Governor Claiborne H. Jackson of Missouri was an eager Secessionist. He had called his legislature into session and guided its deliberations to call a convention that would consider secession. But Missouri was seriously divided and its division ran far back in history. There had been ardent supporters of Thomas H. Benton, and equally ardent opponents who took John C. Calhoun as their mentor. There were Germans in the commercial life of St. Louis and they were tinged with abolitionism. There were proslavery planters in the valley of the Missouri River, who had pushed up the valley into Kansas, when the opening of that area dramatized the issue of slavery in the territories. There were old Whigs like Edward Bates, heirs of the old Jacksonian Democracy like Congressman Frank Blair, new

---

[11] W. B. Bate to Isham G. Harris, Aug. 11, 1861 (Isham G. Harris Collection, Tennessee State Historical Society, Nashville).

radicals like the rising newspaperman B. Gratz Brown. Missouri's politics was confused and its contending leaders were more aggressive than they were able. Its divergent economic groups contended for the direction of the state government. Governor Jackson himself was typical of the mercurial nature of its politicians. At the beginning of the presidential campaign of 1860, he had supported Stephen A. Douglas; before election day he had switched to the Free Democracy of John Breckinridge. The state's electoral vote went to Douglas. Yet, Jackson was disappointed when elections for a convention brought forth a Unionist majority. Nevertheless, he proceeded with his intention to take the state out of the Union, ordered the state militia into camp at St. Louis, and truculently replied to Lincoln's call for troops that the request was "illegal, unconstitutional, revolutionary, diabolical, and cannot be complied with."[12]

But Missouri's Unionists were as active and as apt as Governor Jackson. Congressman Blair, whose brother was in Lincoln's cabinet and whose elderly father had been advising presidents since Jackson, had influenced Lincoln to assign Nathaniel Lyon to command the St. Louis arsenal. The new commander was as fiery an Abolitionist as old John Brown, and he lost no time in taking action. He avowed his intention—or so the Confederate sympathizers alleged—"to reduce Missouri to the condition of Maryland."[13] With Blair's aid he secretly removed the arms in his arsenal across the river into loyal Illinois and then turned, with a handful of regular troops and volunteer units of St. Louis Germans, upon the Missouri militia in Camp Jackson. Ignoring as superficial the fact that they were legally assembled and the flag of the United States flew over the encampment, Lyon forced their surrender and paroled his captives under oath not to take up arms against the United States. Jackson sent an agent to Richmond to beg assistance.

---

[12] *War of the Rebellion* . . . (Washington, 1880-1901), 3, I, 83 (hereinafter *ORA*).
[13] C. E. Cabell to John J. Crittenden, June 26, 1861 (JJCP).

Thereafter a kaleidoscopic series of events kept Missouri in turmoil. General John C. Frémont arrived to take military command of St. Louis and to attempt to organize the radical Germans for his own political ends. Governor Jackson and his Secessionist legislature fled from Columbia, and Nathaniel Lyon lost his life fighting Missouri troops at the Battle of Wilson's Creek. Amid the military confusion and the political maneuvering, a new contribution to the process of political reconstruction was made. In Columbia the Federal troops reassembled the Missouri Convention, which declared the state offices vacant and proceeded to fill the governorship with Hamilton R. Gamble, brother-in-law of Montgomery Blair. The action, paradoxically, was completely in accordance with John C. Calhoun's theory of the convention as a constituent assembly. Thereafter, Lincoln's plan of reconstruction embodied the idea of installing a new governor under military auspices and with whatever popular support he could marshal.

In Kentucky, the third Border State that remained in the Union, the outbreak of war led to a different solution. Kentucky's geographical position was not so crucial as Maryland's, and Lincoln could afford to wait before taking military action to hold her in the Union. Then, too, despite divisions among them, rivals in Kentucky politics were neither as intense nor as aggressive as those in Missouri. Governor Beriah Magoffin was at heart a Secessionist, but his legislature had repeatedly denied either the right or the justification for secession. Tradition, too, made Kentucky the home of compromise and conciliation. Henry Clay had won fame as the Great Compromiser, and John J. Crittenden had made his effort to solve the problems before the country. Magoffin himself, when all hopes of effecting a settlement in Congress had faded, had tried to get the co-operation of the governors of neighboring Ohio and Indiana in making a peace move and a compromise solution. The war-minded governors refused to consider any proposals to avoid conflict, but Magoffin held to his

course. He denounced Lincoln's call for troops as wicked,
but announced that Kentucky would remain neutral.

For the moment Lincoln appeared to accept neutrality,
and in the summer of 1861 Kentucky made its own special
contributions to the growing techniques of reconstruction.
Repeatedly, Union men in Kentucky had advised the President to avoid violence. "Harsh measures from you will
divide the people and Kentucky will be lost," said one. And
Senator Crittenden told General Winfield Scott that Kentucky was "rendering better service in her present position
than she could by becoming an active party in the contest."
Although the administration outwardly respected Kentucky's position, it secretly made steady efforts to undermine Governor Magoffin and the Secessionists. There was
an election coming in August. "We intend to elect an unconditional Union legislature" which would be for coercion,
explained A. O. Bristow to Secretary William H. Seward,
but "to effect this we must be well armed." Arms were
needed to keep down meetings of Secessionists as well as
to discourage Tennesseans from "hopping over to help the
rebels." The arms were soon forthcoming. A New England
Defense Committee and the War Department sent arms to
key men and, by the end of May, General George B. Mc-
Clellan was able to report from Cincinnati that the arms
were encouraging the Unionists and discouraging the Secessionists. The Unionists regarded the distribution as a
"masterpiece of policy" on Lincoln's part. From a Louisville minister Lincoln heard that "neutrality" was only a
Secessionist trick by which Governor Magoffin and ex-
presidential candidate John Breckinridge hoped to promote
secession. Hence, of course, secret means to combat the
plot was not an unneutral or an immoral act. Early in
June, Andrew Johnson, who had waged a fiery and vituperative campaign among East Tennessee Unionists, appeared in Lexington to carry words of cheer and fire to
Kentucky Unionists. But behind the facade of oratory
Johnson was engaged in other work. Already in Cincinnati
a navy lieutenant, William Nelson, was organizing regi-

ments of volunteers for an invasion of East Tennessee, and
Johnson was making plans—acting substantially as Secretary of War for the area—to send the troops across
Kentucky to Cumberland Gap. He was organizing trans-
portation and supply, entrusting men with duties for the
invasion. In Kentucky he was supervising the raising of
regiments and receiving reports on their progress. In
hysteria, Unionists feared that Magoffin had issued secret
orders to muster the state guard to make an open demonstration before election day—"unless thwarted by the vigi-
lance of Union men." There would be use for the troops
Johnson was organizing. And, warned one of Johnson's
advisers, Breckinridge should be watched with "an eagle
eye" and arrested, if he left Washington for Kentucky.
"This is no time to higgle about the niceties or punctillos
when dealing with one of the chief villians of the con-
spiracy." With the ground prepared, when election day
came the armed Unionist took over the polls, non-Unionist
candidates for offices disappeared, and in Louisville, according to a disappointed editor, "several hundred of the Lincoln
soldiers from Camp Holt [at Jeffersonville, Indiana] were
sent over to vote." The Union triumph was complete.[14]

There was one more area where in the first months of the
war important precedents emerged to make up parts of
Lincoln's plan of reconstruction. The western counties of
Virginia, from the Alleghenies to the Ohio River, had long
been unhappily yoked to eastern Virginia Tidewater, Pied-
mont and Valley regions. In the west the Kanawha River
drained a rich valley into the Ohio. North of it, counties
adjacent to the Ohio looked away from Richmond. And if
the "mystic chords" of sentiment did not bind the people to
the Union, the Baltimore and Ohio Railroad tied their commerce to Chesapeake Bay. In Virginia's state convention

[14] T. H. Clay and Amos Lawrence to Crittenden, Jan. 9, 12, 1861
(JJCP); C. W. Clay, Norvin Green, George B. McClellan, and D. P.
Henderson to Lincoln, Feb. 6, March 14, May 30, June 1, 1861;
Crittenden to Winfield Scott and A. O. Bristow to Wm. H. Seward,
May 17, 24, 1861 (RTLP); G. W. Keith and C. F. Mitchell to Andrew
Johnson, July 1, 13, 1861 (AJP). See also E. Merton Coulter, *Civil
War and Readjustment in Kentucky* (Chapel Hill, 1926), 85ff.

the delegates from the west were Unionists and, when the convention reassembled after Sumter and voted to submit the question of secession to a popular vote, part of the western leaders assembled in Wheeling. As in Missouri, there were forceful and aggressive leaders among them— John S. Carlile and Francis H. Pierpont in particular—and they agreed to assemble a convention representing the "loyal" people of the state, if the secession ordinance passed. For years Carlile had been agitating to divide Virginia into two states and he could hardly be restrained from rushing his pet project through without regard to the legal technicalities necessary. Meantime, he made certain that Lincoln, Secretary of War Simon Cameron, and the governors of adjacent Ohio and Pennsylvania promised armed support for the western Virginia Unionists.

Momentarily stopping Carlile from precipitous action, the convention followed Pierpont's more legalistic approach, which had Lincoln's approval. A new convention assembled in June, declared the state offices vacant by the treason of Governor John Letcher and the elected officials, and proceeded to fill the offices, avoiding, said the New York *Tribune*, "the ugly appearance of initiating, on a small scale, the illegal and unconstitutional secession of the Rebel States." And, as one delegate, declaring that Lincoln preferred this procedure, added, "I can see that the design is to introduce the same plan in all the border states . . . as rapidly as the troops advance to establish a similar government." The convention elected Pierpont to the governorship of "Restored" Virginia, the new Governor called the rump legislature into session, and began his administration with funds that Virginia had deposited in the Bank of Weston to build an insane asylum.[15]

The exact lines of apostolic succession between the several Virginia conventions and the governments of Confederate and "Restored" Virginia may have been indistinct, but Lincoln smiled approval on the development. "Congratu-

---

[15] Virgil A. Lewis, *How West Virginia Was Made* (Charleston, 1909), 101-104.

late the people of Virginia," he instructed Secretary Cameron, "on their so soon resuming their relations with the United States." Secretary Cameron recognized Governor Pierpont as commander-in-chief of Virginia troops, and in the Senate Ohio's Ben Wade pushed through a motion to expel Virginia's senators. Radical John Carlile and more moderate Waitman T. Willey, already chosen by the "restored" legislature, took their places. In July Lincoln told Congress that "the government is bound to recognize and protect the loyal citizens of Virginia."[16]

This was, however, as far as Lincoln was prepared to go. With the subsequent movements in western Virginia to divide the state, the President had no connection. Within a few days after the seating of the loyal senators, the "restored" legislature set in motion the steps leading to a new state. In the winter of 1861-1862 a constitutional convention formed the instrument of government for West Virginia, but Lincoln remained only a passive observer of the movement. And, strangely enough, the division of Virginia became no precedent for reconstruction either during or after the war. There may perhaps have been arguments favoring the division of states, readjusting boundaries, or even for rearranging the states of the South into new units, even with new names, to fit either economic realities or political convenience. But no one, social reformer, economic entrepreneur, or political manipulator, seriously proposed readjusting the historical boundaries of the Southern states. Instead, the Virginia contribution to the development of Lincoln's plan of reconstruction was consistent with the lessons learned from Maryland and Missouri.

By the summer of 1861 the experiences of the Border States had given a basic outline to Lincoln's plan of reconstruction. Rejecting any reconstruction of the Union on the basis of a compromise that would have established and

---

[16] Frank S. Reader, *History of the Fifth West Virginia Cavalry* (New Brighton, 1890), 17; *ORA*, 1, II, 723; 3, I, 323-324; Basler, I, 443; Charles H. Ambler, *Francis H. Pierpont* . . . (Chapel Hill, 1937), 113.

guaranteed a duality system, Lincoln had rested his program
on a hope that mystic chords of affection would draw loyal
people back into proper political relations to the government.
To implement the movement he would use patronage to build
a Unionist party. In this support he would use military
power to establish loyal governments among them. The
first steps in Lincoln's plan of reconstruction—the use of
"governments in exile"—had begun to take form. Events
would add refinements to the program.

Chapter II

The War Against the States

Lincoln's Border State policy, his use of troops and even of the patronage to give aid to Unionist elements in overthrowing state governments, and his recognition of governors-in-exile constituted, of course, an invasion of the rights of the states. "I hold that we have no power to make war upon a State of this Union," cried Kentucky's Senator Lazarus Powell, as he opposed giving congressional absolution for Lincoln's unauthorized call for troops. But Congress approved Lincoln's acts and, although Powell's angry cry was echoed thousands of times in the next four years, the war became a war against the states.

Involved in the issue of the war and in the problem of reconstruction was the ancient American doctrine of States Rights. It was a constitutional dogma which dated from the very beginnings of the Republic. The Founding Fathers created a government of delegated powers and when, at the time of the adoption of the Constitution, fears arose that the Federal government would encroach upon the liberties of the people, it was Alexander Hamilton in *The Federalist* (No. 26), who declared that the state legislatures "will always be not only vigilant but suspicious and jealous guardians of the rights of the citizens against encroachments from the federal government, will constantly have their attention awake to the conduct of the national rulers, and will be ready enough, if anything improper appears, to sound the alarm to the people, and not only to be the Voice, but, if necessary, the Arm of discontent." And a few years later, when Hamilton was one of the national rulers, the Virginia House of Delegates, protesting against one of

Hamilton's measures, announced the Doctrine of Sentinelship: "As the guardians then of the rights and interests of their constituents, as sentinels placed by them over the ministers of the federal government, to shield it from their encroachments, or at least to sound the alarm when it is threatened by invasion, they can never reconcile it to their consciences, silently to acquiesce."

Out of the theory that the states were to guard the liberties of the people, Thomas Jefferson elaborated the constitutional theories of the compact nature of the Union. Jefferson knew that democracy was best served by local governments and he believed firmly in keeping power close to the people. The whole rationale of the American Revolution was, in truth, wrapped up in opposition to the absolutism of distant governments, and the Founding Fathers gave but limited powers to the far-off central government. In time John C. Calhoun used the dogma of States Rights to defend the rights of minorities against the aggressive tendencies of the national government. And, although Calhoun's minority was a minority of the opulent, States Rights was still in its essentials a program of those who believed in human liberty against those threats to freedom which they saw in the national government. Even when the South seceded, following the procedures made plain by Calhoun, men cried on liberty to justify their acts. The *Missouri Republican,* on the day that Lincoln called for troops to suppress rebellion, declared that "Alas, it is becoming . . . a question of our own and our children's freedom—a question whether our liberties are secured by laws or whether they are subject to the will, the mere will of despotism." And the *Daily Nashville Patriot,* two weeks later, May 2, 1861, declared that the war "involves two of the prime foundation principles of Republican institutions and liberty—and overruns the theory that all free government is founded on the consent of the people."

The theory of States Rights, however, was not solely concerned with political liberties and the protection of the person against the arbitrary acts of distant governments;

to the rights of states there was economic substance, as well. Except for a few limited areas in which the States surrendered to the Federal government, the states exercised power over property and property relations. It was the states that guaranteed land titles, established boundaries, and defined, under the exercise of police power, the acceptable uses of the land. It was the states which enforced contracts and regulated commerce, chartered banks, established and maintained roads, authorized, financed, and even dug canals, licensed railroads, and lent their credit to support railroads which they not infrequently even owned and operated. Although Chief Justice John Marshall had tried to extend the areas of Federal authority over economic matters, the Supreme Court under Roger B. Taney had consistently refrained from interference with the rightful domain of the states. Until the time of the Civil War, state government regulated the economic life of the people of the United States.

The doctrine of States Rights, at once the bulwark of human liberties and of property, was not a theory confined to the South. There were Northerners too, in 1860, who were devotees of States Rights, and there was no clear-cut division in constitutional theory between the contestants in the war. In the North, too, states protected personal liberty from national aggression. The Personal Liberty Laws of the Northern states, against which the Southerners so bitterly protested, were States Rights devices to protect the liberties of free Negroes and fugitive slaves in the Northern states. And the Republican party platform of 1860, adding paradox to paradox, declared that "The Rights of the States . . . must and shall be preserved," and it added: "The maintenance inviolate of the rights of the states, and especially the right of each state to order and control its own domestic institutions according to its own judgment exclusively is essential to that balance of powers on which the perfection and endurance of our political fabric depends."[1]   Many

[1] William B. Hesseltine, *Lincoln and the War Governors* (New York, 1955), 386.

thousands of old Democrats, who had learned their constitutional principles from Jefferson and Calhoun, were in
the Republican party, and many Northerners, no less than
Southerners, wanted to maintain the rights of the states.

Yet, steadily throughout the war the force of nationalism
battled against the forces of States Rights. It was a battle
that was not fought solely against the embattled armies of
the Confederacy, but was fought in the politics and in the
economics of the North. On the side of nationalism were
the advocates of a high protective tariff, the promoters of
a new system of credit embodied in the national banking
system, the holders of war bonds, the builders, speculators,
and contractors who sponsored governmental subsidies to
a Pacific railroad, the stockholders of nationwide corporations who sought release from state controls—all of whose
interests could be better served by a strong national government. Among the forces too was a war-swollen bureau-
cracy of Federal officeholders and army officers who preferred military command to the competition of civilian life.
With them were men of the trustee tradition in America,
who believed that it was a function of government to exert
its power to improve the morals and the conduct of men.
Slowly, the forces of nationalism re-made the national
economy; the railroads ran to the Pacific as a result of
Federal largess, the giant corporations moved toward mono-
poly, and a benign banking system (whose basis was the
Federal debt) guided the development of the new economic
nation. Slowly, too, the political forces of nationalism
crushed and stifled the political rights of the states.

Perhaps, the growing strength of the national concept
was paralleled by the growth of the idea in the mind of
Abraham Lincoln. In the long years since his death, biographers of Abraham Lincoln have given various interpretations of his personality and his character. Some have
followed the lead of some of his contemporaries and por-
trayed him as a "Man of Sorrows," a great humanitarian, a
noble martyr to the great cause of human freedom. Some,
echoing others among Lincoln's contemporaries, have seen

him as an uncouth clown, a cracker-barrel humorist, a
teller of stories that would disgrace a barroom. There were
Democrats in his day who likened him to a baboon and then
pretended to be shocked by his vulgarity. There were
members of his own party who could not understand a man
who could read a chapter from Artemus Ward as a preface
to a serious discussion. Charles Sumner, a senator who had
been refined rather than educated by Harvard College and
by long years among the elite of Boston, was mystified by
the man who illustrated his penetrating observations on
human conduct with yarns from the folktales of the hinter-
land. What the biographers have too frequently overlooked
in their interpretations of Lincoln, and the thing that many
of his contemporaries never understood, was Lincoln's
capacity for growth. Bemused by the aura of greatness that
surrounds him, bedazzled by Lincoln as the symbol of the
nation that he made, they have dealt with him as a super-
human figure, a god raised up from the prairie, and pictured
him as big in Springfield as he was in that last tragic hour
in Ford's Theater. They have failed to see that Lincoln
the man possessed the rare human trait of being able to
grow, to learn from experience, and to mature in mind
under the strict tutelage of events.

Perhaps, no place is Lincoln's growth better illustrated
than in his evolving concept of the nation. Between the
dates of his two inaugurals he underwent a tremendous
change in the understanding of his problems. Unconsciously,
the transformation was revealed in his vocabulary. In his
first inaugural address he dealt at length with the nature
of the Union. In a sense, of course, he was talking about
the problem of reconstruction. Twenty times he referred
to the Federal Union. It was, he said, "perpetual," it would
"endure forever," it was older than the Constitution, it was
"more perfect" and it could not be destroyed. Repeatedly,
he used the word "Union" as the synonym of the country,
and he closed with the hope that the *chorus of the Union*
would yet swell. Not once did Abraham Lincoln declare
that the United States was a nation. In July, 1861 he sent

his first message to Congress, explaining the argument against secession and asserting that his purpose was to save the Union. Little more than a year later, in August, 1862, he replied to Horace Greeley's "Prayer of Twenty Millions" in the finest statement of his program. "The policy I 'seem to be pursuing' as you say, I have not meant to leave anyone in doubt. I would save the Union." Again and again in this short letter he repeated the phrase "save the Union." But he also declared that his mind was not crystallized. "I shall adopt new views so fast as they appear to be true views."[2]

It was fifteen months later, at the dedication of the Gettysburg Cemetery, and after having met and scotched the hydra of States Rights scores of times, that Lincoln showed that he had adopted new views. "Four score and seven years ago our fathers brought forth on this continent a new nation," he announced—a far cry from what he had said only two score and seven months before. At his inauguration he had talked of the American Revolution, declaring that a Union had been formed by the Declaration of Independence, matured and continued by the Articles of Confederation, and further matured and made more perfect in the Constitution. But in the first inaugural, Lincoln had been concerned with *saving* the Union. Now at Gettysburg, he was convinced that a new nation had been brought forth and he was "highly resolved that this nation, under God, shall have a new birth of freedom." Henceforth, Lincoln spoke little of the Union, often of the Nation. By his second inaugural he used the Union only in a historical sense, referring back to the situation in 1861 : when he spoke of the present or the future it was in terms of the nation. The change in Lincoln's vocabulary was a reflection of the revolution that had occurred in the minds of the American people.[3]

Essentially, Abraham Lincoln was a revolutionary leader,

[2] Basler, V, 388-389.
[3] *Ibid.*, VII, 17-25; VIII, 332-333; William B. Hesseltine, *Lincoln's Problems in Wisconsin* (Madison, 1952), *passim.*

and the cause that he led was a revolutionary one. In a very real sense Jefferson Davis, the constitutionalist, was defending the ancient system against the new forces that had seized control of the apparatus of the government. As the head of those discordant forces, Lincoln faced the tasks of a revolutionary leader—the assertion of his own supremacy over his rivals, the harmonizing of opposing groups, and the furnishing of moral leadership for the revolution. Only a pragmatist, capable of phrasing the ideals of the revolution in moral terms while shifting his course with the necessities of the moment, could have made the revolution a success. It was a revolution that not only destroyed forever the substantive economic rights, but also the political rights of the state governments and, in the process, destroyed as well many of the ancient rights of free men which the states had been dedicated to defend.

In three areas the growing power of the national government struck telling blows at the rights of the states and injured basic human and civil rights. In the suspension of *habeas corpus,* in military conscription, and in the interference of the military in elections, the revolutionists of the 1860's overthrew basic American traditions. To some extent the developing processes of reconstruction in the Border and Southern states served as pilot plants for the assault on the states, and, in turn, the war against the states colored and transformed the processes of reconstruction.

The writ of *habeas corpus* was an ancient English device to prevent imprisonment without due process of law. The United States Constitution provided, negatively, that it might not be suspended except in cases of rebellion or invasion, and the clause was placed among the powers of Congress. It was never determined whether Congress or the President should exercise the right of suspension. In the Confederacy, where the Constitution was more strictly interpreted, the Congress jealously guarded its rights and prevented Jefferson Davis from making such wholesale proclamations of suspension as he desired and recommended. But in the North, in the absence of any clear definition, the

President, and military officers acting in the name of the President, suspended the writ, arrested men, tried them by court martial, and executed the sentences imposed by military commissions. Early in the war Lincoln ordered the writ suspended in Maryland and, under the suspension of the writ, members of the Maryland legislature, suspected of Secessionist sympathies, were lodged in jail. Chief Justice Taney protested, wrote an opinion freeing a prisoner from a military prison, and saw his pronouncements ignored by the local commander. No case involving a suspension of the writ came before the Supreme Court of the United States during the war, but state courts declared that the writ of *habeas corpus* could not be suspended in the states. The Pennsylvania court so held, and the Supreme Court of Wisconsin, which had once presumed to declare the Fugitive Slave Act unconstitutional, was unanimous on the subject. The Wisconsin case grew out of the attempt to draft citizens into the militia. Lincoln had called on the governors for troops and the day after the preliminary Emancipation Proclamation he had ordered the governors to make the draft under the suspension of the writ. The attempt to carry out the order produced riots along Wisconsin's lake shore and the Governor arrested 150 men involved in resisting the enrollment officers. The men appealed to the Supreme Court, which declared that the President had no power to suspend the writ, to declare martial law in Wisconsin, or to subject civilians opposing the draft to courts-martial. But the national authorities could not permit such defiance of authority. Immediately, United States Senator Timothy Howe wired the judges to suspend action until he arrived. With the support of the War Department the Senator appeared, argued the case, and persuaded the judges to reverse their decision. Secretary of War Edwin M. Stanton thanked the Senator with "exceeding joy." And, he added, "accounts from all parts of the country show that the national spirit is growing stronger and stronger."

The cases that got into the civil courts, or even those that were dealt with by formal courts-martial, were few in

number. For the most part the assaults on personal liberty
took the form of arbitrary arrests. Thousands of persons
were arrested, mostly on the eve of elections—and without
exception they were Democrats—held for a few days until
the votes were counted, and released without explanation.

The blanket explanation for the arbitrary arrests was
the alleged activities of secret societies, pledged to the
support of the Confederacy. The name of these imaginary
societies was legion but the most commonly used was the
Knights of the Golden Circle. In the fevered imagination
of some of the neurotic governors of the Middle West, the
Knights of the Golden Circle was plotting constantly to
overthrow the government, seize the banks of the Ohio,
release Confederate prisoners, furnish aid to the enemy,
and vote the Democratic ticket. Richard Yates, governor
of Illinois, was in a constant frenzy over the dangers that
lurked in the southern Illinois counties of "Egypt." Democrats charged that Yates was a drunkard and that he was
always near to delirium tremens. If that were true, the
snakes that Drunken Dick saw in his delirium were Copperheads. He never lost a weekend without a new scare from
Egypt and without having numerous communications, most
of them illiterate, which regaled him with stories of plots,
disaffection, and even armed rebellion in these southern
counties. Yates constantly warned the Washington authorities of the dangers. Once, he sent General John M. Palmer
to Washington to demand that troops be sent to protect the
state. Lincoln listened to Palmer, told him a story, and
dismissed him with the simple question, "If we can't trust
Illinois, whom can we trust?" and Stanton, hearing of the
dangers to Illinois, pronounced the rumors "damned non-
sense."

When no "knight" of the Golden Circle was ever identified and no single fact about the existence of the order ever
brought to light, the military commander in St. Louis, General W. S. Rosecrans, dug up information on the existence of
the Order of American Knights. The General reported that
there were 13,000 members in Missouri and 140,000 in

Illinois. Lincoln sent John Hay to investigate, read his private secretary's report, and decided that it was as puerile as the Knights of the Golden Circle. Then, Governor O. P. Morton found the Sons of Liberty in Indiana. From the beginning of the war Morton had seen hostile Kentuckians lurking in every shadow along the banks of the Ohio and he had constantly called on the national administration to protect the state. Lincoln thought Morton the "skeerdest" man he had ever met and dismissed the matter, but Morton and his provost marshal arrested 2,600 men in a couple of weeks and eventually they sent an agent-provocateur to work among the Democrats. The agent succeeded in getting a handful of men to sign up with the Sons of Liberty, and the exposure of the actual existence of such an order was skillfully timed for the eve of an election.

A substantial number of the arbitrary arrests were of newspaper editors—and among the citadels of liberty that tottered and fell in the course of the war was freedom of the press. From the beginning Democratic editors appraised each passing event with a critical and partisan eye and told their readers how the Republicans rejected compromise for party advantage, how they prolonged the struggle for predatory ends. For the most part the Democratic journals struck a pose as the defenders of the Constitution against the illegal usurpations of Abraham Lincoln and his minions. A few of them, notably Samuel Medary's *Crisis* in Columbus, Ohio, perceived the economic currents that underlay the struggle and pointed out how the rights of the states were being destroyed to make room for industrial interests in control of the national government. The Democrats protested against making the war into a crusade against slavery.

Against these protesting voices the government fought with both propaganda and violence. In the war-fevered imaginations of Republican spokesmen all the Democratic papers which did not abandon their principles and their party were Secessionist sheets and their traitorous editors were "wily agitators" and pro-slavery apologists for Jefferson Davis. Against such vermin all right-thinking, high-minded, and "government-loving" citizens must take drastic steps.

By early 1861, within a couple of weeks of the disaster at Manassas, the attack of the decent citizens against the traitorous press began. A Federal marshal in Philadelphia seized the office of the *Christian Observer*. In West Chester, Pennsylvania "unidentified persons" wrecked the office of the *Jeffersonian*. In New York a Federal grand jury named five papers "which are in the frequent practice of encouraging the rebels." Promptly, the Postmaster General denied the papers the use of the mails and Secretary of State William H. Seward ordered the arrest of an editor.[4]

Subsequently, there was no cessation of suppressions by military authority, barring papers from the mails, arbitrary arrests of editors, and mob attacks on newspaper offices. By the end of the war the military had suppressed more than thirty papers, had barred as many more from the mails, and had arrested four score editors, publishers and reporters. Usually, such arrests came in the small hours of the morning, with a detachment of soldiers awakening the editor in his home and carrying him off without explanations or without suggesting his destination. In addition, mobs destroyed half a hundred newspaper offices and plants, threatened others, and beat, tarred, and feathered, and even murdered, editors. For the most part soldiers constituted the core of the mobs, and always the local military authorities professed themselves unable to apprehend the offenders.

By the close of the war the consistent harassment by reproofs, censorship, temporary suspensions and seizures of issues, in addition to mob action and military arrests, had had its effect. Editors who were carried off to prison usually remained there until they had taken oaths of loyalty and given pledges to support the administration. They returned to their wrecked presses with a new disposition to guard

[4] Robert S. Harper, *Lincoln and the Press* (New York, 1951), 115-116.

their language. Freedom of the press, however, along with States Rights, was one of the casualties of the Civil War.

Yet, all of these scares about secret societies and all the charges that editors were giving aid and comfort to the enemy gave justification for arbitrary arrests, and played definitely into the hands of partisans. Using the secret societies as an excuse, the apostles of nationalism organized secret societies of their own. The Union Leagues and the Strong Bands—"Dark Lantern Societies," Editor Medary called them—kept watch on Democrats and traitors and with arms in their hands struck terror into the hearts of States Rights oppositionists.

The second area in which the forces of nationalism struck a blow at States Rights and incidentally at an ancient human liberty, was in the effort to conscript men into the armies. From the beginning of the United States the disciples of liberty had been opposed to a large army and fearful of militarism. During the War of 1812 some of the New England states interposed the power of the state against the effort to conscript men into the military service. When the Civil War began, the principle of forced military service, already familiar in the tyrannical governments of Europe, was undreamed of in the United States. The first troops called by the Federal government were militia, and they were furnished by the states. Then President Lincoln called for volunteers and Congress created a volunteer army, a national army, but it was raised by the states, bore state designations, and was commanded by officers appointed by the state officials. However, as the war proceeded, it became evident that state officials were unequal to the task of raising sufficient troops. The first men to enter the army thought that war would be short—a ninety-day picnic for the militia—but within a year after the first battles the citizens lost their initial enthusiasm for the bloody business of war. The casualty lists mounted and caution checked the response to patriotic appeals. By the summer of 1862 the governors reported that they were having difficulty in meeting the repeated demand for more and more troops.

Cautiously, they suggested that the Federal government draft men into the army. They were surrendering states' rights before a national emergency—but politicians as they were, they suggested that the Federal government rather than the state governments do the drafting. But Lincoln insisted that the states should continue to raise the men— that the governors should act as recruiting officers for the national armies. In August, 1862 he called on the governors for 300,000 militia, ordering them to draft the men, if they could not get them otherwise.

Faced with necessity of drafting their own constituents, the governors looked for another source of troops and they took up the Abolitionist demand that Negroes should be used. The slaves of the South should be freed, armed, and allowed to fight for their own freedom. Under the pressure of the governors Lincoln yielded a little—enough to issue the preliminary Emancipation Proclamation—and to permit the enlistment of Negro troops, but he did not relax the pressure on the governors. The day after the proclamation Lincoln suspended the writ of *habeas corpus* and ordered the governors to force men into the militia. Early the next year Congress passed an act for national conscription. It was an act designed to force the governors to raise troops for the "volunteer" army. The national government drafted few troops in its own name, but the act reduced the states to administrative units in the raising and maintenance of the national army.

The third area in which the principle of nationalism won victories over states' rights was in Federal military interference in elections. This, too, began in Maryland, where it was justified on the strategic ground that the government could not risk having disloyal men elected to office so close to the national capital. It was continued in Kentucky and Missouri, where Federal troops patrolled the polls, arrested Democratic candidates for office, and generally discouraged the casting of disloyal votes. In 1862 it was the army-controlled votes of the Border States that overcame Democratic victories in the Northern states and enabled the Republicans to retain control over the House of Representatives.

By the middle of 1863 Lincoln was prepared to extend the system which had operated successfully in Kentucky, Missouri, and Maryland to the states of the North. The necessity for such an extension was clear: the Democrats had shown surprising strength in the elections of 1862. Indiana and Illinois had elected Democratic legislatures, and a constitutional convention dominated by Democrats had assembled in Illinois. In Indiana Governor Morton had prorogued the legislature and, refusing to call it into extra session, had run the state without new appropriations. He had collected taxes based on old and expired laws and he had been sustained by funds from the national treasury. He had become as completely dependent on Federal favor as Francis Pierpont was in his residual state of "Restored Virginia." In the spring of 1863 Democrats won local contests in Ohio and looked forward to carrying the state in October.

Leading the Democrats was Congressman Clement L. Vallandigham, a warm supporter of Stephen A. Douglas, who had not, like Douglas, held Lincoln's hat at the inauguration of the Republican revolution. A severe critic of the war measures of the administration, Vallandigham had taken a stand in favor of the lost liberties of the people. He returned to Ohio to continue his criticism as an active candidate for the governorship. His success might have done much to stay the steady course of the war against the rights of the states. But commanding in the Department of the Ohio was Major General Ambrose E. Burnside, an ardent Radical from Rhode Island. Burnside announced that the habit of declaring sympathy for the enemy would not be tolerated in his department, set spies to take notes on Vallandigham's speeches, arrested him, and sentenced him to imprisonment. Embarrassed by the enthusiasm of his subordinate, and fearful of the reactions to the high-handed arrest and sentencing of a prominent political leader, Lincoln commuted the sentence to banishment to the Con-

federacy. But Vallandigham made his way from the Con-
federacy to Canada and conducted his campaign against the
Republican candidate, John E. Brough, from Windsor,
Ontario.

On the eve of election day, thousands of Democrats were
seized by the army. On election day the offices in Washington were almost forced to close and business was at a stand-
still as the government employees from Ohio went home to
vote. More than the officeholders, however, were necessary,
and there were soldiers there from the armies. Units from
the armies in Tennessee and in Virginia went home, osten-
sibly to recruit men to fill the vacancies in their ranks, but
actually to stand guard at the polls and to vote the Republican ticket.

A story came out of the election. That evening Abraham
Lincoln went to the War Department to listen to the returns.
About ten o'clock, seated beside the telegraph operator, he
asked to get in touch with Brough. "Brough, what is your
majority now?" wired Lincoln. "Over 30,000," answered
the Ohioan. At midnight Brough replied, "Over 50,000,"
and before dawn, "over 100,000." Lincoln arose from beside the operator. "Glory to God in the highest," he wired
Brough. "Ohio has saved the Nation." It would have been
a more accurate interpretation, if Brough had exclaimed,
"Thank God, Lincoln has saved Ohio."

It was little more than a month after the election in Ohio
that there was a special election to fill a congressional seat
in Delaware. The little state was nominally Democratic, and
it was scarcely more than nominally a slave state. In 1861
its elderly Governor William Burton, firm in the Democratic
faith, had refused to furnish troops when Lincoln had
called for them. It was not, however, because he objected.
It was, he explained, because Delaware had no militia law.
Federal troops were organized in Delaware without the
consent of the chief executive and the legislature, and
Delaware alone of the slave states in the Union furnished
no organized units to the Confederate armies. But there

was little question that Delaware would send another Democrat to replace the congressman who had died.

The election was on November 19. The day before, Federal troops, commanded by Brigadier General Robert Schenck of Ohio, moved into the fairgrounds at Dover. The next day they were at the polls, inspecting ballots, and passing through the lines of bayonets only those who had Unionist tickets in their hands. The result was the election of a Republican to the vacant seat in Congress.[5]

On the same day, within a hundred miles of the busy soldiers, Abraham Lincoln arose to make a speech. He had come, invited but unwanted, to a ceremony which had designed to emphasize the importance of the states. As the state governors had been reduced to mere recruiting agents for a national army, as the economic power of the states had been submerged in the larger economics of the nation, as the states had no longer been willing or able to stand in their ancient sentinel boxes to warn of national encroachments on personal liberties, the governors of the states had turned to representing themselves as the "friends of the soldiers," and to making efforts to insure that the troops from their states were well cared for, their wounded properly hospitalized, their sufferings in field, camp, and hospital ameliorated by state agents. As evidence of this concern, the states had combined to purchase the burial ground at Gettysburg, where the casualties of that great battle had been laid to rest. To the meeting, designed to glorify the states, came Abraham Lincoln to speak of the nation. He did not say that, four score and seven years before, the founding fathers had brought forth thirteen sovereign states. He said that they had created a nation, and he dedicated his audience to the support of national principles.

That day, in Delaware and at Gettysburg, the war against the states received its fullest expression. The national government had demonstrated on that battlefield its power to defeat the armed and combined might of the states. The

[5] Henry S. Conrad, *History of the State of Delaware* (Washington, 1908), I, 203-204.

rights of the states, and indeed, many of the ancient rights of free men, were buried, and the men who had fought for and against the rights of the states lay in neat rows in a national cemetery.

Three weeks after his appearance in Gettysburg, Abraham Lincoln announced his plan for amnesty and reconstruction. In the background of that plan was the war which the national government had carried on against the states, and the offer which the President made was not an offer to restore the old Union. It was an offer to the Southern people to re-order their political structures and to re-take their places in the new nation which had supplanted the old union of the states.

CHAPTER III

The Military Governments

On November 8, 1863 President Abraham Lincoln issued his Proclamation of Amnesty and Reconstruction. It was a scant three weeks after the Ohio election, but already Lincoln's concepts of the nation, rather than the old Federal Union, had taken final shape. Yet, the developments in the war which the national government waged against the states were only part of the background of the pronouncement. Another part grew more directly out of the experiences and experiments with military governors in the conquered areas of the South.

The experiences in the Border States in the spring and summer of 1861 had set the pattern. In Missouri and in Virginia the disloyal Confederate governors had been replaced, with the aid of arms, by loyal governors and by Unionist legislatures. In the summer of 1862 the precedent had been followed, when Kentucky's Governor Magoffin had resigned in favor of Thomas Bramlette. The administration looked forward to reconstructing the states by the simple process of extending the authority of Pierpont and Gamble over disaffected people and areas.

It was a logical and natural extension of the idea of the loyal governor replacing the disloyal one for Andrew Johnson to become the military governor of Tennessee. In many respects Johnson was the Tennessee counterpart of Virginia's Pierpont. He was a Democrat adhering to the ancient doctrine of States Rights, but opposed to the leading elements of his party, a Unionist who vigorously opposed secession, and a representative of a disaffected section out of tune with the dominant sentiment in his state. But Johnson, unlike Pierpont, joined the Radical faction of the Republican party and spouted fiery denunciations at the South's leaders.

But for the exigencies of distance, which prevented Federal aid and the quick actions of the Tennessee and Confederate governments, the East Tennessee mountaineers might have followed the course that their Virginia neighbors took. Or, in another aspect, had Virginia's Governor John Letcher been as apt and as alert as Tennessee's Governor Isham G. Harris, he might have seriously hampered the activities of the western Virginians and have forestalled the division of his state. In Tennessee, as in Virginia, the mountain counties felt themselves unequally yoked with the other sections of the state. They had ambitions for their own economic development which ran counter to the state's dominant economic interests and they had long agitated for separation into another state. Yet circumstances prevented the formation of a new state and permitted Unionist leaders from East Tennessee to manipulate the processes of reconstruction.

In 1860 Unionist sentiment was strong in Tennessee. John Bell, the Constitutional Union candidate for the presidency, was an old Tennessee leader, and he carried his state in the election. The success of Lincoln in the campaign caused no excessive disturbance in the Volunteer State. As South Carolina hurried into convention, the Memphis *Enquirer* warned that secession was "only a mad-man's remedy" for Southern wrongs. In Knoxville, on the opposite side of the state, "Parson" William Gannaway Brownlow vehemently forecast in his *Whig*: "You may leave the vessel . . . you may go out in the rickety boats of your little state and hoist your miserable *cabbage leaf* of a palmetto flag; but depend upon it, men and brethren, you will be dashed to pieces on the rocks."[1]

But Governor Harris was as ardent a Secessionist as

[1] Avery O. Craven, *The Growth of Southern Nationalism, 1848-1861* (Baton Rouge, 1953), 380-381.

Missouri's Governor Jackson. On January 1, 1861 the legislature met at his call, heard him outline the list of outrages the North had committed against the South, and set an election for a convention early in February. During the next month Senator Andrew Johnson and Congressmen Thomas A. R. Nelson and Horace Maynard joined old Whigs and Constitutional Unionists in campaigning for the Union. The voters turned down the convention by a vote of 68,282 to 59,448, but even this was not fully indicative of Tennessee sentiment. Unionist candidates for the convention polled 91,803 votes to 14,794 for avowed Secessionists. Only cotton-growing West Tennessee voted to join the South.

In such a situation Lincoln's policy of using the patronage to bolster the active Unionist elements in a border state might have been successful. Although there was talk of a cabinet post for John Bell, and many of Lincoln's advisors urged him to seek out the counsel of the Unionist leader, Lincoln made no gestures toward the Constitutional Unionists. Nor did he consult Democratic Unionists like Andrew Johnson on matters of patronage. Johnson, after all, had voted for Breckinridge. Perhaps, Lincoln counted too heavily on the Unionist vote in February or, perhaps, he discounted too heavily the determination and influence of Isham G. Harris.

Governor Harris was unwavering, and sentiment in Tennessee had quickly changed with the firing on Fort Sumter and Lincoln's call for troops. John Bell condemned Lincoln's policy. Although he disapproved of secession and advocated neutrality and favored joining Kentucky in a neutral bloc, he began to waver. Harris reassembled the legislature, which drafted an ordinance of secession to submit to a popular vote. Immediately the campaign of January was re-enacted, but this time the results were different: only 47,000 voted for the Union, while 105,000 favored the ordinance. But East Tennessee, casting 30,000 of the minority votes, remained in the Unionist column.[2]

_____

[2] Katherine Born, "The Unionist Movement in East Tennessee During the Civil War and Reconstruction Period" (unpublished M. A.

During the campaign, Unionists held a convention at Knoxville to declare that "the President of the United States has made no threat against the law-abiding people of Tennessee." The convention drafted a memorial favoring the division of the state—and appointed a day for reconvening should the ordinance pass.

But the Unionists of Tennessee were not so fortunate as their neighbors to the north. The Knoxville convention did not have even so tenuous an appearance of legality as did the Wheeling meeting, nor did it have the protection of bayonets from neighboring Ohio and the blessings of Lincoln. Instead, Confederate bayonets guarded the polls on election day and discouraged Union voters. Already Governor Harris had entered into a military alliance with the Confederate government, and Jefferson Davis's administration was acutely conscious of the importance of the railroad through East Tennessee that united Virginia to the Lower South.[3] The region was as vital to Davis's government as Maryland was to Lincoln's, and for all his devotion to constitutional practices, Davis was as willing as Lincoln to meet a dangerous situation with military force. When, on June 17, the adjourned convention assembled in Greeneville, the nearness of Confederate troops prevented its delegates from taking revolutionary action. Although they proclaimed that the counties of East Tennessee were the legal state of Tennessee, and that they would remain neutral, they could not declare the state offices vacant. Instead, they petitioned the legislature at Nashville for a division of the state. The legislature, of course, took no action, and in the next few months state and Confederate troops arrested and imprisoned Unionist leaders in East Tennessee.

thesis, University of Wisconsin, 1933), 19-24; William B. Hesseltine, *The South in American History* (New York, 1943), 459-460; Joseph H. Parks, "John Bell and Secession," *East Tennessee Historical Society Publications*, XVI, 30-47 (1944) hereinafter *ETHSP;* James G. Randall, *The Civil War and Reconstruction* (Boston, 1953), 253.
[3] Edward C. Smith, *The Borderland and the Civil War* (New York, 1927), 288-289; Born, 27-35, 63-66.

While East Tennessee remained under Confederate bayonets, Lincoln belatedly planned a rescue mission. Under the urgings of Andrew Johnson and Horace Maynard, the President became concerned about East Tennessee's Unionists. He pressed on the War Department the importance of taking Cumberland Gap, he authorized the arming of Unionists in Kentucky, and he gave approval to the organization of troops for the rescue mission. Once, fully assured that General Don Carlos Buell, commanding at Cincinnati, would march in to aid them, Unionists burned railroad bridges and cut Richmond off from the Southern heartland. But Buell did not move, and Confederate authorities tracked down the bridge burners for summary punishment and picked up more Unionist leaders in the process. The people of East Tennessee logically concluded that the Federal government had betrayed them. Buell's failure to move had prevented a division of the state, perhaps. Had Federal forces captured East Tennessee first, the situation might have strengthened the separate statehood movement.

Instead of in East Tennessee, where Unionist sentiment was strong, Federal forces—under Ulysses S. Grant instead of Buell—moved into Middle and West Tennessee. In February, 1862 Grant took Forts Henry and Donelson, and Confederates withdrew from Nashville—taking Governor Harris and his government into exile. Grant immediately occupied the capital and within a few days Lincoln appointed Andrew Johnson to be military governor of Tennessee.

Fort Henry had hardly fallen, when the White House began to have visions of uniting the Unionists of Tennessee. Lincoln's secretary, John G. Nicolay, wrote his fiancée that the Union sentiment in all parts of Tennessee was most gratifying, and "from present indications we shall almost be enabled to hold that state by merely liberating public opinion from the thrall of terrorism in which it has been suppressed." And from Tennessee, thought Nicolay, "we can easily reach every one of the cotton states." He was indeed partly correct. If there was any part of the Confederacy where Unionism was strong, it was Tennessee.

Yet neither Nicolay, the President, nor any of Lincoln's advisors in the North understood that Southern Unionism was a complex of many attitudes and opinions, and a mere release from the thrall of the Confederate government was not sufficient to re-establish Federal authority.[4]

Among the varied elements that composed Southern Unionism, there were those based upon economic, upon political, and upon sentimental considerations. There were Southern men who had commercial ties with the North, and others who hoped that Northern victory would bring them benefits in trade and commerce. There were others who saw the Federal government as the ultimate protector of property—even property in slaves—and who feared for their possessions in the midst of war. "The love of the Union only comes after the love of their property," observed a Belgian citizen, who had traveled in Kentucky and Tennessee and whose adverse comments on Southern Unionism had been sent by the Belgian minister in a friendly gesture to Secretary William H. Seward. A Tennessean, observing the situation from the distorted perspective to be obtained in Nicaragua, came to the conclusion that Andrew Johnson's course "may yet save slavery for the South," while Jefferson Davis and Robert Toombs were "more likely to break down a government than build it up."[5] And there were East Tennesseans, moreover, who were particularly conscious of the potential wealth that lay in the mineral resources and abundant water power sites of their mountains. Parson Brownlow, foreseeing an industrial development for Knoxville, had long proclaimed himself an "Alexander-Hamilton-Henry Clay-Internal Improvement-Whig." He believed that industrial development and the long-sought canal route around Muscle Shoals would come better under the United States than under the Confederate States of America.

[4] Carman and Luthin, 215-216; John G. Nicolay to Theresa, Feb. 17, 1862 (John G. Nicolay Papers, Library of Congress, hereinafter JGNP).
[5] John P. Heiss to Andrew Johnson, March 12, 1862 (AJP).

Other Unionists there were with political ambitions, who saw greater opportunities for themselves in the United States than in the Confederacy. Not least of these was Andrew Johnson, the only Southerner who refused to quit the United States Senate, when his state seceded. Clearly, his long opposition to his Southern colleagues made his future in the Confederacy dubious, while his opportunities for success in the United States were particularly bright. In the early months of his Unionist campaigns his mailbox was filled with letters holding out the presidency of the United States to him. His Unionism, his Democratic antecedents, his Radical affiliations—all the things which were to make him particularly available for the vice-presidential nomination in 1864—were equally promising avenues to the Union Party's nomination for the highest office. Two months after he became military governor of Tennessee, Ohio's John Sherman held out to him the White House as a reward for success in Tennessee. "The honest people of the country want somebody to rally about," advised Sherman. "The waste, fraud, folly, weakness mingled with cruelty, jokes mixed with tragedy of many high in power sickens me. I want honesty, sincerity, and fidelity to friends in a new leader." In fact, added Sherman, had it not been for the unifying force of the war, the Lincoln administration would be "Tylerized in three days." Johnson might indeed have expected the presidency, and many a lesser Unionist could have looked forward to rewards in the Federal government.[6]

Finally, in addition to economic reasons and political ambitions, there were other forces—social forces—that animated Southern Unionists. Yeomen farmers in the plantation areas and men of the mountains opposed the South's cotton aristocracy and could be as scornful of Southern "chivalry" as any Yankee artisan. Many, too, were bound by ties of sentiment—even by those mystic chords of memory to which Lincoln appealed in his first inaugural—

---

[6] John Sherman to Andrew Johnson, Apr. 27, 1862 (AJP).

and clung to the Union with patriotic devotion. Among them were others who believed that liberty and freedom, dogmas made dear by the American heritage, were to be preserved only in the Federal Union.

Equally important as the complex, even confusing and conflicting elements in Southern Unionism, there was in Tennessee as well as in other Southern states, a growing disaffection for the Confederacy's military management and civil activities. The Confederate soldiers who withdrew before Grant's advance from Donelson were in an ugly mood when they reached Nashville. As they arrived in the Tennessee capital, Governor Harris and a substantial portion of the leading Confederate citizens left. The troops, reported one observer, "were so mad that they committed all excesses possible," and did an estimated $5,000,000 worth of damage. They fell upon the "magnificent place" of Andrew Ewing's, fed their horses in its parlors—using the sofas for feed troughs—and saying "Damn him. He got us into the trouble and now is the first man, except the governor, to run away!" When they had withdrawn—and "every editor left, every Methodist preacher left"—the city was desolated. It looked, indeed, like "Sabbath in cholera time."[7]

That Andrew Johnson was the best man to harmonize the conflicting Unionists and win over the disaffected Confederates was open to doubt. Assistant Secretary of War Thomas A. Scott visited Nashville as soon as the Federal troops entered and quickly reported to Lincoln that Johnson was not the best man to send. He had made many enemies. Indeed, feeling against him was so bitter that there would be danger of his assassination. On the other hand, Scott advised, General William Campbell, equally as staunch a Unionist, but with a gentler disposition and a less fiery vocabulary, would give general satisfaction. Campbell would be particularly acceptable to the wealthy classes who had been through sheer necessity aiding the rebellion. But

[7] Reese W. Porter to Andrew Johnson, March 1, 1862 (AJP).

Lincoln ignored Scott's advice and sent Johnson as military governor. His precise duties remained unknown. Secretary Stanton authorized him to establish necessary offices, suspend the writ of *habeas corpus,* and "exercise all the duties of a military governor" until the loyal inhabitants should have organized a civil government in conformity with the Constitution of the United States.

Andrew Johnson immediately appeared in Nashville. During the nine months since the secession of Tennessee he had remained in the Senate, acting with the emerging Radical group of Republicans rather than with the Democratic minority, and losing no opportunity to denounce the Confederate leaders and to threaten leading Confederates with punishment and the confiscation of their property. He voted for the confiscation acts and became an active member of the Radical-dominated Committee on the Conduct of the War. There was reason indeed for the fear that he would be despotic.

On March 13, 1862, the evening after his arrival in Nashville, Johnson addressed the citizens. The sole purpose of the military government, he explained carefully, was to aid in returning the state to its former place in the Union. Private citizens who would renounce disloyalty and return to their allegiance would be welcomed. There would be no confiscation of property of loyal citizens and no effort to interfere with domestic institutions. A few days later Johnson issued a formal proclamation, setting forth his interpretation of the situation. The state government had disappeared, the executive had abdicated—"the great ship of state, freighted with its precious cargo of human interests and human hopes, its sails all set, and its glorious old flag unfurled, has been suddenly abandoned by its officers and mutinous crew, and left to float at the mercy of the winds, and to be plundered by every rover of the deep." In that situation—which was probably as confused as Johnson's metaphors—he had been appointed governor. He invited fellow citizens to occupy the offices, promised protection of property to those who had been "loyal through the dark night," and asserted that he would punish "intelligent and conscious treason, but no retaliatory or vindictive policy" would be followed.

Neither the speech, the proclamation, nor Johnson's early acts were reassuring to either Unionists or disaffected Confederates, and few rallied to his support. He began by demanding that the mayor and council of Nashville take an oath of allegiance. They refused, alleging that as corporation officers they were not liable to take oaths not prescribed by law. Johnson removed them and the new city officers whom he appointed imposed the oath on all municipal employees and upon schoolteachers. Soon arrests began. Squads of soldiers, appearing in the dark hours of the morning, seized seven prominent citizens of Nashville, and throughout the state within the lines of the Union armies the search for Secessionist leaders went on. Within six weeks Johnson ordered the *Times* and the *Banner* suppressed, and soon he imported a Kentucky Unionist to edit the new *Daily Union*. He closed the *Patriot* and the *Gazette* and seized both the Methodist and Baptist publishing houses for spreading disloyalty. He ordered six ministers to take the oath and when they refused he exiled five of them to the Confederacy. Soon after, he arrested a former governor, a judge of the chancery court, and the president and the cashier of the Union Bank of Nashville. He sent warrants to military commanders in various parts of the state to be used at the officers' discretion.[8]

The arrests and suppressions, arousing popular sympathy for the victims and exciting widespread apprehension, did nothing to bring out any hidden Unionist sentiment. As soon as he took office, Johnson began to hear from Confederate soldiers in Northern military prisons who were eager to take oaths of allegiance. "We voted for the Union and the constitution as free men," declared a group of prisoners in Camp Morton, Indiana, "but the time came

[8] Charles H. McCarthy, *Lincoln's Plan of Reconstruction* (New York, 1901), 17-23; Clifton R. Hall, *Andrew Johnson . . .* (Princeton, 1916), 42-44.

when we had to lay our mouths in the dust and dared not speak our sentiments." They had joined the Confederate Army to keep from being drafted and to save their property from depredations by their Rebel neighbors. Tennesseans in prison at Camp Chase and Johnson's Island in Ohio added their pleas, while a distraught mother from Standard City in the fifth "destrick" wrote a "fue lines" to "Mr. Ander Jonsin" to "lete you no of my trobles the lord hath give me my sone and now he is takin a way a prisner at chicargo he was a union boy . . . he never went out tel the malisha was calld and compeld to go." Johnson asked for and obtained control over Tennesseans in Union prisons but he delayed taking action for their release and restoration until he and his agents could be completely sure that each applicant was completely free of all Confederate taint. The reaction in the prisons was one of disgust. "I petitioned in good faith to take the oath of allegiance," complained one prisoner, but the delay demonstrated that the "government has no confidence in any man south of Mason and Dixon's line." "Great God!" he cried, "How do they expect to restore the Union . . . ? Do they expect to keep a corporal's guard upon every farm in Tennessee . . . ? Much as we love the union of our fathers and much as we wish to see it restored, common sense would teach us that it can never be done unless Tennessee can be received back in the union upon an equal footing with her other sisters of the republic. 3-400 citizens in Camp Chase petitioned in good faith . . . but instead of having the hand of brethren extended to us, we are denounced as traitors, murderers and thieves. Is this the spirit with which we who are knocking at the door for admittance are to be received? Then all hope is lost and we are already slaves."[9]

Unionist civilians within the Confederate lines fared no better than the unfortunates who had been constrained to enter the Confederate Army. Johnson seemed determined to force from them professions of unswerving loyalty and

[9] Unidentified to Andrew Johnson, June 6, 1862 (AJP).

to purify the Union party before proceeding with the organization of a civil government. In fact, he seemed more determined to create a political party under his own control than to institute a state government. Hoping to arouse the Unionists, he sponsored a series of mass meetings at which speakers assured the audiences that the purposes of the government were conciliatory. There would be no confiscation of property. Out of a Nashville meeting there grew a Union Central Committee which set about to organize patriotic sentiment in the state. Partly to see who were Unionists, Johnson permitted a "test election" for a circuit judge. The voters chose the anti-administration candidate, and the Governor duly gave him his commission—then he arrested him and kept him in prison while his defeated opponent took the office!

Yet for all the protestations that property rights would be respected, Unionists and neutrals had no evidence they could believe the promises. Even before Nashville fell, Tennessee loyalists had set up a clamor to get compensation for property lost to the Secessionists. One fugitive from Maryville had lost two trunks on the railroad. He not only wanted to be recompensed, but he proposed that the property of Rebels should be seized for the larger purpose of paying the costs of the war. If, he explained, Rebels kept their wealth, it would not be ten years before they would cause trouble again. "They ought to be made to feel that there is a strong government, strong because it is just and beneficent to its loyal citizens, but terrible to all its enemies." Another refugee hoped that Secessionists of Middle Tennessee should not "go upwhipt of justice," while a clerk in the Treasury Department advised Johnson to remember that "there is a long list of accounts to be settled in Tennessee."[10]

The conduct of neither Johnson nor the military authorities gave any assurance that property rights would be respected. Unionists and disaffected Secessionists looked with similar horror upon the Yankee speculators who

[10] F. A. Reeve to Andrew Johnson, March 4, 1862 (AJP).

swarmed after the army, armed with trade permits from the army and the treasury departments, and who dealt with Secessionists as well as Unionists. By the middle of 1863 General Grant told Secretary Chase that "no honest man has made money in West Tennessee in the last year, while many fortunes have been made."

Especially was there no protection for slave property. Early in May six Union citizens appealed to Johnson against the depredations of Wisconsin's Norwegian regiment. The soldiers of the Fifteenth Wisconsin were prowling the countryside, carrying off slave women and children, and sending off large numbers on transports. Colonel Hans C. Heg kept two Negroes belonging to Union citizens as his personal servants. Johnson's only response was to make a Fourth of July address, reiterating his doctrine that traitors must be impoverished and arguing the general proposition that Southerners had repudiated debts to Northerners amounting to ten times the value of the slaves that Yankees had stolen in the South. In Nashville, the military impressed slaves of Unionists to build the fortifications of the city and then turned them loose when the forts were completed. One owner got a military order to recover two female slaves whom soldiers had enticed away, but when he got them in a carriage, soldiers bore down upon him, freed the women, and carried the owner off to the penitentiary.

At the same time that irregular proceedings against Rebels caught Union men, Johnson's government was negligent in setting up a system by which Unionists could recover damages from either the military or from Secessionists. Johnson delayed establishing courts in Memphis after the city fell, and the only justice was that administered by military commissions. Yet, as Unionists with claims against Secessionists pointed out, keeping civil courts closed protected the latter against judgments. Federal authorities in Memphis seized the property of disloyal men and courts could use their power to compensate loyalists. In Middle Tennessee county and circuit courts operated under military protection, but military courts operated independently, and

friction between them became acute. General W. S. Rosecrans set up a Board of Claims, which carefully accorded
its awards to faithful and loyal citizens, but its judgments
were not always those which the civil courts would support.

While the Unionists in Tennesse were thus confused and
evincing a growing hostility to Johnson and the military
establishment, Lincoln's Emancipation Proclamation came
to complete the rift in their ranks. Many Unionists were
slaveholders and had relied on the repeated assurances that
property would be respected and protected. The change in
the purpose of the war brought dissension among the Union
men. Colonel W. B. Campbell reported to Johnson that the
proclamation would "produce most serious difficulties, and
embarrass the suppression of the rebellion." There was,
in truth, danger of revolt in the army. Kentucky troops
would not sustain the order and Campbell even suspected
that Kentuckians permitted General Bragg to escape after
his defeat at Perryville because of lack of enthusiasm for
an abolitionist war.[11]

Despite the unfavorable reactions to the proclamation
and before any readjustments would be made, new assurances given, or the remnants of the divided Unionists re-
organized as a political party, Lincoln began to insist that
congressional elections be held in occupied districts. In
October he sent commissioners to Tennessee to arouse sentiment for the elections. The commissioners found Johnson
reluctant and the military authorities generally unsympa-
thetic and uncoöperative. Despite the unfavorable auspices,
Johnson yielded to Lincoln's wishes, set December 29 as
the date of elections, and appointed election judges to see
that only desirable Union men voted. But the opening of
the campaign encouraged the dissenters. At Bolivar, in

---

[11] Kentuckian B. F. Buckner, an officer in a Union regiment, was
seriously affected by the proclamation. To his financeé, Helen
Martin, he wrote, Nov. 8, 1862, "It is a most abominable infamous
document and falsifies all his [Lincoln's] pledges both public and
private . . . . No Kentuckian can have any heart for this contest."
On December 2-3 Buckner resigned and hoped he would not be
dismissed, but his resignation was not accepted (mss. in University
of Kentucky Library, Lexington).

Tennessee's Tenth Judicial District, a meeting adopted resolutions which fell "short of the loyal and patriotic dec-
larations which the occasion required." In fact, the meeting
solemnly proclaimed that the time was ripe for Tennessee
to be represented in congress, because "we believe it better
to take part in governing ourselves than to be governed by
others." Moreover, the meeting declared itself in favor
of an honorable and speedy peace and a restoration of the
Union on the old terms. There was also a resolution to
instruct representatives to work against the Emancipation
Proclamation and to secure laws compensating masters for
losses of slaves caused by the United States Army. The
advantages of a short campaign were obvious and Johnson
hoped that the twenty days he had allowed for the contest would be too brief a time for the anti-emancipation
Unionists to organize. Fortunately, the Confederates
coöperated with him. On election day General Nathan B.
Forrest's cavalry raided the districts and the polls in one
district remained closed. Some time later a would-be
congressman appeared in Washington, but the House of
Representatives refused him the seat he claimed. Under
the circumstances, Forrest's raid may have been a mistake.
Tennessee's congressman elected at that moment might
have done more damage to the Union cause than Forrest's
hurrying raiders!

No small part of Johnson's troubles sprang from the
presence of military forces in Tennessee with other duties
than administering the government. Generals Henry W.
Halleck, Grant and Buell were engaged in an active campaign against the enemy and could hardly afford to take
time to organize a state government. Even as Johnson
arrived in Nashville, General Buell protested to General
George B. McClellan against the hasty establishment of a
civil government. It was, he thought, "injudicious at the
time." "It may not be necessary at all," he added. The
War Department instructed Johnson that the military would
aid him in his duties, but Buell added his own proviso that
complying with any requisitions which involved troops must

depend on the plans of the army. Johnson told Lincoln that petty jealousies among the generals made it impossible for him to perform his duties.

In the fall of 1862 disagreements between Johnson and Buell led to the assignment of General William S. Rosecrans to Nashville. The change brought no improvement in relations. Rosecrans was as hysterical a radical as Johnson and the provost marshal whom he appointed for Nashville soon had the citizens aroused. By January, 1863 even Johnson was angry. He complained to Rosecrans, but the General smugly replied that he would only see that justice was done. Johnson took his complaint to Washington where Halleck, now "general-in-chief" and principal advisor to Lincoln on military affairs, proposed that Johnson be given direct command of troops. But Rosecrans refused to coöperate. Then rumors spread that Rosecrans and his provost marshal were speculating in cotton, and Johnson credited the stories and reported them. Angry correspondence between the General and the Governor only led to Secretary Stanton's sending a commission to investigate. Eventually, despite Rosecrans' protests, the provost marshal was forced out. The troubles contributed nothing to the conciliation or pacification of Tennessee but it left Johnson with a permanent distaste for military tribunals and military men as agents of reconstruction.

As problems grew with the military, Johnson had other problems. When East Tennessee fell into Federal hands, the Unionists there began to organize—and to divide between administration supporters and opponents. Parson Brownlow went back to Knoxville to re-establish his virulent newspaper—now renamed the *Whig and Rebel Ventilator*—and to rally Unionists in his own behalf. In West Tennessee Johnson met a clamor for the organization of militia forces which could aid in ferreting out Secessionists and suppressing guerillas. But Johnson also learned that dissident factions in Memphis proposed, as soon as elections for state officers were permitted, to organize an opposition party and rally around William B. Campbell for governor. In the

meantime, the Johnson forces organized a Union League
which proposed that the militia be organized and all Southern sympathizers exiled. "Old party feuds" were breaking
out, reported one of Johnson's supporters, in all parts of
the state.[12]

Probably, Johnson wanted to delay elections until he could
be sure that they would result in pro-emancipation victories,
and until he could organize a Union party that could carry
the election. Lincoln, however, was impatient. Early in
September the President told Johnson that Tennessee was
cleared of armed Rebels and it was the "nick of time" for
setting up a loyal government. But, warned Lincoln, this
re-inauguration must not result in the choice of enemies of
the Union. "Let the reconstruction be the work of such
only as can be trusted for the Union. Exclude all others."
Then, Lincoln added, Johnson should "get emancipation
into your new state government." Reluctantly, hesitatingly,
Johnson proceeded with the work of holding a constitutional
convention for Tennessee.

This was on the eve of Lincoln's Proclamation of Amnesty
and Reconstruction. By that time Lincoln had had more
than a year and a half of experience with military government in the Volunteer State. He had instructed Johnson
to establish a government on the base of the loyal people
of Tennessee. He had, however, made no objection to Johnson's arbitrary arrests or to his purging of officeholders.
He had advised no conciliatory policy and had not inter-
fered with the military courts. In the meantime, Johnson
had taken actions which tended to dissipate Unionist sentiment and to bring confusion into the ranks of the Unionists.
Both Lincoln and Johnson were politicians and they had
thought first of the creation of a political party which
would be sure to place the offices in the hands of pro-
administration men.

The Tennessee situation was not alone in the background
of Lincoln's Proclamation of Amnesty and Reconstruction.

[12] Hall, 93.

Shortly after Johnson's appointment to Tennessee, Lincoln selected military governors for Louisiana, North Carolina, and Arkansas. At the moment, Federal forces had gained a foothold in each of these states and the new military governors had followed the troops. In each state there was reason to believe that there was considerable Unionist sentiment that needed only to be aroused and organized in order to repeat the processes already under way in Missouri and Virginia. In two of the states, however, there was not enough area and population under Federal control to make a beginning at the restoration of civil government. Governors Edward Stanley in North Carolina and General John S. Phelps in Arkansas failed to make headway and Lincoln substantially abandoned hope of getting any kind of reorganization started in their states.

The story in Louisiana was different. There the Unionist sentiment was perhaps less pronounced than in many other Southern states, but what there was, was concentrated in the commercial city of New Orleans. Merchants and shippers of the city, concerned with the handling of trade through the mouth of the Mississippi, might well have looked ruefully at the disruption of commerce which secession and war might entail. However quiet they may have been, they feared the destruction of the city's commercial facilities, and when a Federal force and fleet approached in March, 1862, they made haste to surrender the city before its levees, wharves and warehouses were subjected to bombardment. Upon the base of such commercial interests, a Unionist movement might conceivably have been based, but the Federal commander, Benjamin F. Butler, made no effort to conciliate the commercial leaders. Butler had already made minor contributions to the developing techniques of reconstruction. In Maryland he had conquered Annapolis and the distracted City of Baltimore and had restored order with ruthless dispatch. At Fortress Monroe he had declared fugitive slaves to be contraband of war and had put them to work. He had brought to New Orleans a well-developed sense of the dramatic possibilities of a military governor, a sardonic sense of humor, and a complete conviction that the wealthy, the slaveholders, and the existing leaders of the city government were Secessionists and traitors at heart.

Along with Butler went Colonel George F. Shepley of the Twelfth Maine, a Democrat who had been, a scarce two years before, a delegate to the Charleston convention where Butler had persistently voted for Jefferson Davis as the party's presidential nominee. Like Butler, Shepley had turned into a Radical Republican. In June, 1862, at Butler's instance, Shepley became military governor and then, a month later, he had received promotion to a brigadier generalship. His instructions had the same vague words as Andrew Johnson's in Tennessee, but Shepley never attempted to assert his own authority or to quarrel with the military. He was a mere clerk for Butler and his actual role was circumscribed by Butler's whims. Butler himself gave little attention to the eventual establishment of a civil government but, like Johnson in Tennessee, he attempted to build a political party as a preliminary to the creation of a civilian government.

Ignoring the possibility of enlisting the support of the wealthy planters and traders of Louisiana, Butler attempted to win the support of the hitherto neglected lower classes. He put laborers to work on public works and paid them from levies upon the richer Secessionists. This frank and open wooing of the lower classes contributed to driving Unionists and neutrals into the arms of the Southerners. Corruption, too, characterized Butler's rule and became an obvious symbol of Federal victory. There was nothing in the Butler régime to induce Secessionists to return to their old allegiance.

When complaints of Butler and his officers reached Washington, Lincoln sent Reverdy Johnson to investigate conditions. But, he instructed the agent, if the people objected to Butler, the way for them to avoid the "inconveniences" arising from military occupation was "simply to take their place in the Union upon the old terms." More elaborately, he explained to Cuthbert Bullitt a few days later, the people who petitioned for protection of persons and property had "but to reach forth their hands and take it." If in good faith they inaugurated the national authority, set up a state government, and became loyal citizens, the army would protect them. "They know how to do it," said the President, and the army would withdraw as soon as a state government could dispense with its presence. "The state can then, upon the old constitutional terms, govern themselves to their own liking."

Whatever the meaning of this promise, Lincoln was anxious for action. After the Emancipation Proclamation he eagerly sought approval from the South. In November he urged Governor Shepley to hold congressional elections— but, he explained carefully, "I wish it to be a movement of the people of the districts and not a movement of our military and quasi-military authorities there." There had been fears that Federal officers, or hangers-on, might run for Congress. "There could be no possible object in such an election," said the President. "We do not particularly need members of Congress from there to get along with legislation here." But "what we do want is conclusive evidence that respectable citizens of Louisiana are willing to be members of Congress." A "parcel of men" elected by bayonets would be, he thought, "disgusting and outrageous" and Congress would be justified in refusing them seats. "Do not waste a day about it."

Under such stimulus Shepley and Butler supervised an election in two districts in and about New Orleans and a handful of voters sent Michael Hahn and Benjamin F. Flanders to Congress. They took their seats—not without opposition—in the House, but their election was hardly evidence that a substantial body of respectable citizens were willing to participate in the Federal government.[13]

[13] McCarthy, 38, 39; John G. Nicolay and John Hay, *Complete Works of Abraham Lincoln* (New York, 1905), VIII, 79-81; Willie M. Caskey, *Secession and Restoration in Louisiana* (Baton Rouge, 1938), 55-56; Hans L. Trefousse, *Ben Butler, The South Called Him Beast!* (New York, 1957), 132-133.

Two weeks after the election General Nathaniel P. Banks succeeded Butler as military commander. Shepley stayed on and Banks attempted to undo Butler's work of antagonizing the citizens. He tried to encourage them to reopen their factories, to renew farming operations on their sugar, rice, and cotton plantations. He organized the Negro laborers and sought means of inducing them to remain at their homes and cultivate their fields. As soon as Hahn and Flanders took their seats in February, 1863, Banks gave encouragement to the formation of Union Leagues which began to hold weekly meetings and to agitate for the complete inauguration of a loyal state government.

Lincoln watched the movement and carefully avowed his abstention from interference. "While I very well know what I would be glad for Louisiana to do," he told Banks in the summer of 1863, "it is quite a different thing for me to assume direction of the matter." He wanted a new constitution adopting emancipation, but his restraint gave no stimulus to the formation of a Union party. Throughout the summer of 1863 Banks and Shepley worked at cross purposes. Banks was a moderate, eager to establish peace and conciliate the enemies of the government. Shepley was a radical, anxious to fasten Butler's Unionists recruits in control of the state. Finally, in November Banks held an election, and the Constitutional-Union Party—which bore no relation to the Bell-Everett party of 1860—carried all the offices. The voters chose J. L. Riddell governor and sent three men to Congress. The vote was small. One congressman went to Washington with the approval of only 156 constituents! The congressmen got temporary seats and they heard Lincoln, in his annual message of 1863, explain his Proclamation of Amnesty and Reconstruction. But a credentials committee soon ousted them, because they represented no substantial number of voters and their credentials had been signed by a governor who had not been regularly elected—or even inaugurated.[14]

[14] McCarthy, 51.

Yet, even this result was better than the record in North Carolina and Arkansas—better even than Andrew Johnson's record in Tennessee. Lincoln's policy of political reconstruction under military auspices, the careful nurturing of Union sentiment by military commanders, had borne little fruit. Clearly, there was a need for a more definite pronouncement on the modes of reconstruction.

The moment seemed appropriate for announcing an offer of amnesty. Southern morale had been declining steadily with military reverses. First, the fall of Vicksburg and the failure of Lee's expedition at Gettysburg in July had sharpened criticism of Jefferson Davis throughout the Confederacy. The victory at Chickamauga in September had been followed by bickering and dissension among Confederate military commanders and eventually by the defeat at Chattanooga. The Confederacy had been cut in two, while no effort to win back a single point of Union advance had been successful. The elections of 1863 would bring an angry group of anti-Davis congressmen into Richmond.

Sensing the situation, General Rosecrans in Chattanooga wrote Lincoln, proposing an offer of amnesty. At the moment Rosecrans was surrounded by a Confederate Army which had cut off his food supply and was patiently watching for Federal troops, badly beaten at Chickamauga, to starve. Either totally unaware of his own precarious position or trying to put the best face on his predicament, Rosecrans turned to politics. "If we can maintain this position in such strength that the enemy are obliged to abandon their position," said Rosecrans unrealistically, and "the elections in the great states go favorably, would it not be well to offer a general amnesty to all officers and soldiers in the Rebellion?" It would, he continued, give moral strength to the Union and weaken the Confederacy.

There was a hidden barb in Lincoln's reply. Already, in Nashville and in St. Louis, Rosecrans had proved an unreliable observer and a poor guide. "I intend doing something like what you suggest," answered Lincoln, "whenever the case shall make it appear ripe enough to have it accepted in true understanding, rather than as a confession of weakness and fear." For the moment he waited. Then the elections, thanks to his intervention, went well enough in the great states, and the soldiers in Chattanooga, now commanded by Grant, "obliged" the enemy to abandon his position on Missionary Ridge. An offer of amnesty to the Confederates would no longer appear a confession of weakness.[15]

Clearly, too, the time had come to make a new program of reconstruction. The military governors were having at best mediocre success, and a new plan was needed. Late in August General H. W. Halleck saw his opportunity to put in an additional stroke for army control. The question of reconstruction in Louisiana, Mississippi, and Arkansas, he told Sherman, would soon come up. It was, he admitted, a difficult matter, but the length, even the success, of the war depended on it. "If the President will consult opinions of cool and discreet men," Halleck believed that the question could be solved. The President, thought Halleck, should "receive the advice of our generals who have been in these states, and know much more of their condition than gassy politicians in Congress." At Halleck's suggestion, Banks had written. Sherman should also write. "Consult with Grant, McPherson, and others of cool, good judgment," advised Halleck, "and write me fully as I may wish to use them with the President."

The General was right in believing that the time for a decision was near, but Lincoln was not prepared to take the cool good judgment of the generals. On December 8, the day Congress reconvened, Lincoln announced a new program for reconstruction. As if he had grown weary of searching for competent Unionists to organize the rebellious states, the President prefaced his announcement about reconstruction with an offer of amnesty. Making exception of high-ranking officers in the army or in civil life, or men who had once taken an oath to support the constitution and then

---

[15] Basler, VI, 498; *Memoirs of General William Tecumseh Sherman* (New York, 1891), I, 363.

joined the rebellion, or those who had been specifically declared outlaws for mistreating colored troops, Lincoln offered to all Confederates an opportunity to take an oath of allegiance. The oath prescribed a pledge to support, protect, and defend the Constitution and the Union, and to abide by all acts of Congress and proclamations of the President concerning slaves. It was a relatively simple oath and its takers would receive protection of their persons and property—except slaves.

The amnesty was a preface to a plan of reconstruction. Basing his actions on the premise that subversive elements had seized the state governments and that loyal people desired to re-inaugurate loyal governments, Lincoln proposed that whenever 10 per cent of the voting population of 1860 should have taken the prescribed oath, that 10 per cent might re-establish a state government which, if republican in form, he would recognize as the true government of the state. There was, however, one proviso: the name of the state, its boundary, and its subdivisions should remain unchanged. Lincoln had no taste for separate statehood movements which had already split Virginia and threatened Tennessee. Virginia—Pierpont's "Restored Virginia"—was omitted from the proclamation.

On the day of the proclamation Lincoln sent his message to Congress. In it he attempted to explain his program. Nothing, he said, was attempted beyond what was amply justified by the Constitution. The provision about maintaining the boundaries of the states would "save labor and avoid great confusion." Further, the President explained, some states were ready for action but remained inactive for want of a plan. His plan was offered as a "rallying point" that would hasten action. Of course, the admission of congressmen, Lincoln explained, remained with the respective houses. His was not, he assured the congressmen, an exclusive plan: he would approve any other method which proved effective.[16]

[16] Basler, VII, 50-53.

The plan of reconstruction which Lincoln set forth in his proclamation and explained to Congress was deceptively simple—as remarkable for its omissions as for its provisions. It rested on the assumption that the recognition of a state government was the exclusive function of the executive. It rested, too, on the assumption that reconstruction was solely a political function. Hidden in it was the background of the war which Lincoln was waging against the states—a war which was making him the master of his party and of the nation. But the unspoken implications of Lincoln's deceptively simple plan of reconstruction were not lost upon his opponents in Congress. There was a social program of reconstruction and a mounting economic interest that might not be fulfilled under Lincoln's proclamation.

Chapter IV

Social Experiment and Economic Penetration

Back of Lincoln's proclamation outlining his second plan of reconstruction, developing while the military governors were struggling to find and organize a loyal party and inaugurate loyal governments, and while Lincoln was steadily gaining a position of mastery in the Northern and Border States, another program was evolving. Back in the winter of 1860-1861 the discussion of compromise proposals had revealed a sentiment which would tolerate no adjustment that would permit slavery to survive. For a dozen years at least the abolitionist element in the Free Soil and Republican parties had been agitating, not only against slavery but also against the whole economic and social fabric of the South, seeking to solidify Northern political power in order to destroy Southern influence in politics, in legislation, in the total life of the nation. The struggle to prevent the extention of slavery into the territories was but one phase of a consistent, many-fronted campaign against the South. By the winter of the secession crisis the Abolitionists had succeeded in making slavery into a symbol of Southernism, in identifying the anti-slavery crusade with a crusade against the economics, the politics, and the culture of the land of Dixie. Any compromise that would secure even a breathing spell for slavery met their intransigent opposition. They not only favored a war for the Union, but they also prepared as well to make the war an agency for reconstructing the South—and the nation.

In their thinking and in their willingness to use governmental power, even military force, to effect a moral reform, these Abolitionists, who became the Radical faction of the Republican party, were acting and thinking in accordance with a tradition as old as America. Stemming out of the Puritan ethic, bolstered by the theological concepts of Calvinism, theirs was the tradition of the trustees—the elect of God who lived under a compulsion to regulate society for the greater glorification of God. The trustees were the stewards, especially selected to preside over society and believing that those whom God favored he prospered. Throughout the first half of the Nineteenth Century men of the trustee tradition had worked with inspired zeal to reform and order American society according to divine wishes. They had formed societies for moral reform, for temperance, for Bible reading, for Sabbath observance, for peace, for spreading morality by tracts, and for the abolition of slavery. They had deplored the settlement of the West by discontented elements from eastern society and they had formed an education association to foster the training of ministers for them, a missionary society to promote Protestant worship among them, a tract society to furnish them with uplifting literature which stressed above all things the payment of debts and financial honesty. The trustees had looked askance at the hordes of immigrants who had poured into America, and promptly showered missionaries and Bibles and tracts upon the newcomers. Nor had the trustees hestitated to use the coercive power of the state, when moral suasion brought slow results. They agitated for Sunday closing laws, tried to force their moral literature into public schools, enacted a prohibition law in Maine, and worked to get similar laws adopted in other states. The men of the trustee tradition would not hesitate to use the war to abolish slavery and to remake Southern society on a moral model.

The prospect was clear in the first days of the war. The conflict was but two weeks old when Henry W. Halleck, then the organizer of distant California's militia, warned

Maryland's Reverdy Johnson that the North would become "ultra anti-slavery, and, I fear, in the course of the war will declare for emancipation and thus add the horrors of a servile to that of a civil war." If Maryland, Halleck thought, could be kept in the Union, then slavery would "still be recognized and protected under the constitution and the door kept open for a compromise or reconstruction if either should become possible."[1]

Although Halleck's prescription had no effect, his diagnosis and prognosis were correct. The course of the Abolitionist Radicals was paced by Massachusetts' Senator Charles Sumner, a consistent and virulent opponent of the South. From the beginning Sumner was determined that the war should be made into an abolitionist conflict. Lincoln kept on good personal terms with Sumner, and the Senator—who enjoyed practicing French and discussing literature with Mrs. Lincoln—was regularly at the White House. Steadily, he prodded Lincoln to "Strike at slavery." On the day after the First Battle of Manassas, he called at the White House to insist, unrealistically, that the moment for the blow had come. Lincoln failed to agree, but in and out of season Sumner drove toward his objective. In October, 1861 he told the Massachusetts State Republican Convention that "slavery is our Cataline, being to this war everything, inspiration, motive power, end and aim, be-all and end-all." This, stated the Boston *Advertiser*, October 4, 1861, was an attempt to make the Republicans into a "John Brown Party," warning that "neither men nor money will be forthcoming," if the people were convinced that abolition and not the defense of the Union was its object. But criticism could not deter the abolitionist. "I propose no crusade for abolition," he ingeniously told a critic. He would save the Union. He merely insisted that "the Union can be preserved only by striking at slavery." Abolition was not the object of the war—it was merely one of its

[1] James G. Wilson, "General Halleck, A Memoir," *Journal of the Military Service Institutions of the United States*, XXXVI, 553 (1905).

agencies. The day after giving this explanation Sumner appeared at Cooper Union to deliver an all-inclusive diatribe against the peculiar institution. Slavery was, as all could see, "the ruling idea of the rebellion." It "marshalled these hosts," "stamps its character upon officers and men," "speaks in the word of command and sounds in the morning drum-beat," "digs trenches," and "points the cannon." Sumner had succeeded in making complete the integration of slavery and the South.[2]

"Mr. Sumner deals exclusively with the theory of war," commented the New York *Times*, and added that the Senator had no practical method of conducting it. The Massachusetts Abolitionist voted for the confiscation acts of 1861 and 1862, but he explained that he did so only because it was a method of emancipation. "To give freedom is nobler than to take property," he remarked sententiously. On the other hand, he was diligent in advancing the civil rights of Negroes. He forced the Washington street railroads to abandon segregation in their cars. He threw his weight into the scales in favor of using colored troops and he forced the War Department to give them equal pay with white soldiers. He opposed the organization of Montana Territory on the ground that the law made no provision for suffrage for Negroes. "It is something," he replied to objections that there were no Negroes in Montana, "to declare a principle! The principle is more important than the bill."

As for the reconstruction of the South, Sumner took an eager and early interest. "Assuming complete military success," he asked Francis Lieber, the political scientist in March, 1862, when military success seemed remote indeed, "What next?" Answering himself, he declared reorganization would be next and "the most difficult of all." How, he asked, should it be done? "Will the people cooperate enough to constitute self-government? I have positive opinions here."

The Senator was not asking expert advice. His questions

[2] Edward L. Pierce, *Memoirs and Letters of Charles Sumner* (Boston, 1894), IV, 49.

were purely rhetorical and intended to instruct rather than
consult the great pundit. Subjugation with emancipation
was his answer and, as to the process, his opinion was
positive, indeed. The President had no authority in the
process—no right to appoint governors, institute conventions, supervise elections. These were the functions of
Congress. Moreover, Sumner had no confidence in Lincoln's
ability to find a loyal population that could institute self-
government in the Southern states. Long before Lincoln
proposed to permit oath-taking Confederates to take control, Sumner had determined that Negroes must be given the
suffrage and the work of reorganization confined to them.[3]

Charles Sumner was the most incessantly articulate ad-
vocate of abolition in Congress, but he was not alone. With
him was a group of Radical Republicans—Benjamin F.
Wade, George W. Julian, Joshua Giddings, Thaddeus Stevens, and many another—who were as intense as he in their
determination to make the war a crusade against slavery
and to effect a social reorganization of the South. Controlling the Committee on the Conduct of the War, having
the sympathy of Salmon P. Chase and Edwin M. Stanton in
Lincoln's cabinet, they purged Democratic and pro-slavery
generals from the army and became the official promul-
gators of war propaganda. But for the most part they were
less purists than the Massachusetts Senator. Sumner was
interested in social reform and in the political and constitutional machinery for effecting it. His fellow Radicals
combined economic change with the social reformation, and
sought, more or less overtly, to destroy the Southern economic system.

Even more vigorous than the Radical clique in Congress
were the Union League Clubs of New York and Philadelphia
and the New England Loyal Publication Society. The Union

---

[3] *Ibid.*, IV, 74-79. New York *Times*, March 28, 1861. "I have never
discovered any aptitude for ideas or signs of genius in him," wrote
Amos Bronson Alcott, March 8, 1850. "He seems conventional,
scholastic, commonplace, and owes his reputation mainly to a noble
disposition and a fine person. His attainments are all of the Harvard
cast" (Odell Shepard, ed., *The Journal of Amos Bronson Alcott*
[Boston, 1938], 228).

League was an organization of "true" Republicans whose local chapters, first organized in Illinois and soon spread over the Middle West and across the Alleghenies, served to instill patriotic sentiments and promote patriotic acts in communities, to stir up enthusiasm for the war and above all, to make sure that Republicans rather than War Democrats dominated the "Union" party.

The Union League was, in fact, a party within a party. The metropolitan clubs of Philadelphia, New York and Boston added the further refinement of being gentlemen's clubs, complete with club houses and a varied program of social activities, within them. No small part of their activities was the dissemination of propaganda. Millions of copies of hundreds of pamphlets, essays, speeches, editorials, and "broadsides" containing documents, news accounts, and reports which editors could print in local papers flooded the North, went to soldiers in the army, and even, when possible, to loyal whites and Negroes in the South. The continuous stream of propaganda literature that flowed from the efficiently organized Union League of Philadelphia, and the two Union League-sponsored groups, the New York Loyal Publication Society and the New England Loyal Publication Society, was overwhelming.

Directing the operations of the Union League's club-propaganda machines were leading men of the cities' economic and political life and the contents of the literature reflected their views—Benjamin Gerhard, J. I. C. Hare, Henry Lea, William H. Ashurst, John W. Forney, and Joshua Lippincott of Philadelphia; John Austin Stevens, Jr., Charles Astor Bristed, Sinclair Tousey, George Putnam, Alexander Stewart and Peter Cooper of New York; and John Murray Forbes and Charles Loring of Boston. Some of the more astute thinkers in the nation lent their talents to writing persuasive tracts and essays—Charles Eliot Norton, Francis Lieber, Oliver W. Holmes, Henry Lea and Horace Binney, for examples.[4] They opposed Lincoln's

---

[4] Record Book of George H. Harlow, Grand State Secretary of the Union League of America of Illinois, 1862-1865 (mss. in Union League

assumption that reconstruction was a presidential function. They demanded that the South be treated as a conquered territory and that military government should continue over the conquered districts until sufficient numbers of loyal inhabitants had succeeded in forming a Republican government—no state was to be readmitted to the Union without the liberation of its slaves. They attacked slavery and the plantation system, charging that slavery was a hindrance to Northern progress, a barbarism, and a denial of the perfectibility of man. The spread of national feeling and interest, smooth-flowing trade, travel and emigration, and a homogeneity of American institutions they asserted, were inhibited by the South's wasteful agricultural system. Writing for the Philadelphia Union League, Oliver W. Holmes described the war as a struggle of Southern against Northern nationalism. "The Southerners erected a slave empire while the Northern section of the land was a great variety-shop of which the Atlantic cities are the long-extended counter."

Typical of the Radical Union League's propaganda against the Southern economy and its slave system were

Club of Chicago); *Proceedings of the Grand Council of the Union League of America for the State of Illinois at Its Second Annual Session, September 2, 1863* (Springfield, 1863), 9-10; Gerard E. Morgan to Joseph Holt, Feb. 18, 1862 (Joseph Holt Papers); *Proceedings of the National Convention, Union League of America, Held at Cleveland, May 20 and 21, 1863* (Washington, 1863), 12, 22. See also Clement M. Silvestro, "None but Patriots: The Union Leagues in Civil War and Reconstruction" (unpublished Ph. D. thesis, University of Wisconsin, 1959), 44-60, 122-131; Henry W. Bellows, *Historical Sketch of the Union League Club of New York* (New York, 1879), 11-18; Minutes of the Board of Directors of the Union League of Philadelphia, Jan.-March, 1863, *passim;* Minutes of the Meeting of the Union Club of Boston, Feb.-March, 1863, *passim.*

Gerhard and Ashurst were businessmen; Hare, an outstanding lawyer; Forney, editor of the Philadelphia *Press* and Washington *Chronicle;* Lippincott and Lea, publishers; Stevens, a banker and president of the New York Chamber of Commerce; Bristed, an author; Housey, president of the American News Co.; Putnam, a publisher; Stewart, a merchant; Cooper, a manufacturer and inventor; Forbes, a financier, businessman and railroad speculator; and Loring, a Boston lawyer. Norton was a professor of classics at Harvard College, Lieber a professor of political science at Columbia University, Holmes a famous Boston jurist, Lea a historian, and Binney a Philadelphia jurist.

the remarks of Francis Lieber, who maintained that the continuation of the plantation system with its slave labor would result in the death of the yeoman farmer in the South. Propagandists emphasized the benefits of free labor in a free society and the superiority of the Northern wage system. The New England Loyal Publication Society broadsides featured summaries of extensive surveys and experiments for growing cotton with free labor, made by Edward Atkinson, a member and a leading textile manufacturer. Others described Edward Philbrick's experiment on Sea Island, Georgia, where he used free Negroes to work confiscated plantations. These articles pointed out that Negroes in the South were willing and eager to work for wages and, given this purchasing power, would form a highly potential market for Northern goods.[5]

The Radicals in and out of Congress and among the purposeful propagandists of the Union League clubs found example and precept for their program of reconstruction in the government of New Orleans under Major General Benjamin F. Butler. In May, 1862 the defenseless city, which had relied too heavily on the fleet and fortifications on the Lower Mississippi, surrendered without a struggle and Butler moved in at the head of the occupation troops. As his first act Butler issued a proclamation to all "persons well disposed to the government" of the United States who would "renew" their oath of allegiance. Such persons should receive a safeguard of protection to their persons and property, but "violation of such safeguard will be punishable

---

[5] *Report of the Executive Committee of the Grand National Council of the Union League of America, Dec. 14, 1864* (Washington, 1864), 5; *The Return of Rebellious States to the Union* . . . (Philadelphia, 1864). *Grand Mass Meeting of Loyal Citizens* . . . *March 6, 1863* (New York, 1863), 10-16; Oliver W. Holmes, *Oration Delivered* . . . *Boston* (Philadelphia, 1863), 4-12, 23-25; Francis Lieber, *Slave Plantations and the Yeomanry* (New York, 1863), 5. See also Edward Atkinson to William B. Rogers, July 13, Atkinson to C. E. Norton, July 20, 1863 (Edward A. Atkinson Papers, Massachusetts Historical Society, Boston), and *New England Loyal Publication Society Papers*, No. 90 (Boston, 1865?). Philbrick's letter appeared in the Boston *Daily Advertiser*, July 20, 1863. See George W. Smith, "Broadsides for Freedom: Civil War Propaganda in New England," *New England Quarterly*, XXI, 291-312 (Sept., 1948).

by death." Persons not so well disposed and keeping their
allegiance to the Confederacy were, said Butler, enemies
without rights. All keepers of public property, national,
state, or Confederate would immediately make full report
of their inventory. Otherwise, the inhabitants should, en-
joined Butler, pursue their usual business. Furthermore,
Butler set up special courts to handle all disturbances, dis-
orders, and breaches of the peace, and to deal with all
crimes of an aggravated nature interfering with the forces
or laws of the United States.[6]

That his régime would be harsh and intolerant to Confederates became immediately evident. He seized, tried,
and hanged one over-enthusiastic Rebel who cut down a
newly-erected United States flag. He arrested citizens of
Confederate sympathies, ousted local officers and imprisoned editors, who gave less than wholehearted support to
his régime. He arrested Pierre Soulé, one-time member
of Congress and former minister to Spain, for example, and
sent him off to Fort Warren in Boston Harbor. Soulé, said
Butler, was an active member of a Southern Independence
Association opposed to all restoration of the Union, and the
principal local supporter of the rebellion. "His influence
and social position here render him dangerous."[7] Moreover,
those citizens whom he retained as prisoners in New Orleans
he put in ball and chain and sent to labor on the fortifications. Promptly, the Confederate government began to
consider means of retaliation.

Butler's attacks on the Secessionists of New Orleans were
not limited to arresting Confederate sympathizers. He demanded that banks holding Confederate deposits surrender
them to the United States Treasury—and in specie or in the
notes of Northern banks. The bankers protested futilely
that the funds had been deposited in Confederate money,
but Butler insisted upon his pound of gold. Moreover, the
General soon began to tax individuals and business firms

[6] James Parton, *General Butler in New Orleans* (New York, 1864),
293.
[7] *ORA*, 2, III, 612.

who had aided the rebellion. The funds collected went into a poor fund and Butler soon had the destitute poor, white and black, of the city working on public works and supported by the fines extracted from the Secessionists. Thus did he buy the loyalty of the poorer classes. He proposed, in addition, to bribe the better classes by offering amnesty, assurances of personal safety, and safeguards of property from confiscation. "Men of business and intelligence and planters from the country," Butler told Secretary Stanton, came in every day, asking condonation of past political offenses. If he were permitted to offer amnesty, he went on, he could promise that Louisiana would return to her allegiance within sixty days. But Stanton, content with Butler's treatment of the Confederates of New Orleans, saw no reason to make the process less severe.

Butler's course in New Orleans was far removed from Lincoln's conciliatory efforts to find and organize the loyal population of the South, but it met enthusiastic response from the Radicals in Congress and their supporters in the Union League. The measures designed to destroy the Southern economic system met warm approval, while the organization of a potential new electorate appealed to the ambitions of aspiring politicians. Not least among the latter was Secretary of the Treasury Salmon P. Chase. Butler's administration in New Orleans, the Secretary informed the General, had given "the greatest satisfaction" to all his friends. Lincoln, said Chase, had put Butler in an embarrassing position by having no fixed policy in regard to slavery. But Butler should make his own position clear: "Let it be understood that you are no pro-slavery man." In fact, Chase could find but one admonition to give. Rumors abounded that Butler and his officers had been engaged in "mercantile speculation" and this, thought Chase, sounded the only sour note in an otherwise excellent administration.[8]

Butler's men were indeed engaged in what Chase euphe-

[8] *Ibid.*, 3, II, 162-168; 2, III, 674; 2, II, 173-174.

mistically called "mercantile speculation." In the Confederate vocabulary, they were looting, and Butler was "stealing the spoons of New Orleans." In the idiom of a later generation, they were engaged in "black market" activities. Whatever the vocabulary, they were acquiring cotton and shipping it to the North. At Ship Island Brigadier General Neal Dow, author and principal defender of Maine's prohibition law, diverted a government vessel to carry the contents of several plantation homes to his own house in Portland. Butler's brother, favored by cotton trading permits, grew rich in the Crescent City. The military government in New Orleans was giving a crude but a vivid and well-understood lesson in the economic purposes of reconstruction.

A more complete demonstration, accompanied by quite different problems, came in the Sea Islands off the coast of South Carolina. Here social reform, economic exploitation, and military interests came into conflict as the representatives of each interest strove to put into operation their several concepts of reconstruction. In November, 1861 a naval expedition captured Confederate forts at Hilton Head and Bay Point and a group of islands, including Port Royal, Hilton Head, Saint Helena, Edisto, and Ladies Island, containing 195 plantations and about ten thousand slaves, fell into Union hands. The plantation owners, among whom were the Bernards, Haywards, Rhetts, and Stuarts—names prominent in the social and economic life of South Carolina —fled to the mainland, abandoning both their lands and their people. The situation presented a golden opportunity for the advocates of social reform, and literally a golden opportunity for profitable operations in the highly prized and high-priced Sea Island variety of long staple cotton. Immediately, the soon-to-be-contending forces moved in. The War Department, acting through its generals, faced the problems of governing an occupied area, the Treasury Department came after the cotton, and representatives of radical humanitarian groups came after the souls and minds of men.

The War Department's problems were the simplest and most direct. The naval expedition which had captured the islands included 1,500 men under the command of General Thomas W. Sherman. Sherman immediately took possession of all property, issuing a proclamation inviting the assorted Bernards, Haywards and Rhetts to return and, when they failed to do so, divided the islands into districts under supervisors to manage the plantations, organize the slaves into working parties, and grow cotton. In December the War Department authorized Sherman to organize Negroes into squads and companies for local militia duty. In March, 1862 Sherman gave way to David Hunter, an ardent Abolitionist who had early attached himself to Lincoln's entourage and who had risen beyond his merits because of his alleged influence with the President. Hunter signalized his administration by issuing a proclamation declaring slaves to be free, not only in South Carolina, but in Georgia and Florida as well. Moreover, he attempted to organize a regiment of Negro soldiers and, when the island population showed little interest in relinquishing their new-found freedom for the slavery of military discipline, Hunter began to draft them into the service. His proclamation, however, was as obnoxious to Lincoln as Frémont's earlier one had been, and he rescinded it. When Hunter persisted in the effort to raise Negro troops, Lincoln ordered him replaced. All but one company of Negroes thereupon disbanded. But, then, in January, 1863 Hunter came back to the islands and once again began to force Negroes into the army. The Negroes took to flight. As one supervisor of a plantation wrote furiously, "They were caught last year, they will not be caught again." Another observer—he was William Francis Allen, the man who would later begin the University of Wisconsin's history department—found himself in the garden of a plantation shortly after the word arrived that the draft had begun again. "All of a sudden," he said, "a dozen young men plunged into the woodland. I found soon that two soldiers had been passing, and they thought they were after them sure."[9]

The major objection to the army's activities came from those who were trying to raise cotton. When the troops arrived, they found a large store of cotton, and Secretary Chase immediately sent agents to collect it. Legally, it could be taken under the Confiscation Acts and under the provisions of a direct tax law. Extra-legally, it could be taken because it was available. By June, 1862 Sea Island cotton, gathered at Port Royal and shipped to New York, had brought $726,984, of which more than a half million, after deducting expenses, went into the United States Treasury. In addition to the agents sent to collect cotton Chase sent Edward L. Pierce, an ardent Abolitionist and a close friend (and later a biographer) of Charles Sumner, to undertake the social reorganization of the islands and to grow more cotton. Upon arrival Pierce made a survey of conditions among the Negroes and the customary methods of producing cotton. Optimistically, he reported that he could raise 2,500,000 pounds of cotton a year. He found also that the army had divided the islands into districts, under the direction of superintendents, an arrangment he continued. Each superintendent took charge of several plantations with a foreman on each who could divide the land and assign work according to the wishes of the Negroes. The superintendents promised wages for each hoeing and 2¢ a pound for picked cotton.[10]

The arrangement was simple: its execution proved difficult. The superintendents and foremen found the Negroes unwilling to work. Younger Negroes roamed the islands while older ones lazed indoors and neglected the fields. They had, to the astonishment of the Yankees, no concept of wages, expected provisions to be furnished them, and worked only under compulsion. Pierce reported his difficulties to Chase, but repeated also his continuing optimism

[9] *Ibid.*, 1, VI, 176. William Francis Allen Diary, 111 (Jan. 28, 1864), in Wisconsin State Historical Society, Madison.
[10] *Ibid.*, 94 (Jan. 11, 1864).

and devout determination. If, he said, "a beneficent reform shall be achieved here, the experiment may be anywhere attempted." Hopefully, he explained to Negroes he herded into a church on Ladies Island that Lincoln himself was thinking what he could do for them. The great trouble was that their former masters, who had thought they were lazy, had always cared for them, he added. But now Lincoln had "sent me down here to see if that were so." The superintendents would report to Lincoln. If they were to be free, Pierce went on carefully, all had to work and, if they did not, they would be shut up and deprived of privileges. They should stay on their plantations and raise cotton. If they behaved well, they would get wages, better food, and not have their wives and children sold off—and by and by they would be as well off as white people. The superintendent thought indeed that he was being elementary, careful, explicit and even that he was painting a picture of a desirable future. His words, however, availed little—they could not disguise the fact that freedom, no less than slavery, involved labor.

More than cotton, thought Pierce, had to be derived from the Sea Islands. The Negroes must be educated and taught to become "sober and self-supporting citizens." To realize his aim Pierce appealed to Northern people to send teachers to the islands. For a long time the men of the trustee tradition had been pinning their hopes on the schoolroom. Years before, Horace Mann had won the support of Massachusetts industrialists for a program of public schools by arguing that a properly designed curriculum would instill moral precepts, right attitudes toward property, and a proper spirit of labor in the working classes. Education, in the right hands, was a means of social control. The appeal from the Sea Islands fell on the ears of a people convinced of the efficacy of education. In Boston the Educational Commission for Freedmen (later the New England Freeman's Aid Society), in New York the National Freedman Relief Association, and in Philadelphia the Port Royal Relief Committee (later the Pennsylvania Freedman's Relief Association), each with the blessing of the Union League and radical propaganda groups, sprang into being and furiously collected money, clothing, and books for Negroes. Moreover, they recruited teachers, and early in March 31 men and women left Boston for Port Royal. By summer the number had grown to 93, of whom 19 were women and 74 men. Each received $25 to $50 a month. Soon seven of the first group began classes at Port Royal and surrounding plantations and promptly began sending back reports of the high intellectual capacity of their pupils and of their eagerness for learning. Some of the pupils even paid a tuition fee of 5¢ a week. "I find the people I meet much less degraded than I expected," reported William Allen. "I can only say that their dress is slovenly, although nothing like so bad as among the Irish."

The combination of cotton and culture bore some strange products. The teachers had difficulties with the superintendents of plantations, and both had troubles with the military. The opportunities for speculation were abundant and too tempting for some members of each group to resist. The soldiers on the islands pilfered the plantations, especially for fresh foods, and made problems for the superintendents. The first cotton agents resented the missionaries and the teachers—"damned Abolitionists," said the agents. The superintendents, in turn, deplored the missionaries—"sent here because they are fit for nothing else." Clergymen took government stores that were to be sold at low prices to the Negroes, sold them at high prices, and pocketed the profits. The Negroes were getting varied lessons in the operation of the Northern economic system. Their wages, which were to instill respect for the new ways, were paid irregularly and some officials pocketed the Negroes' money. No man, sighed Pierce, not even the best, "should be put into the position where there should be such a conflict between his humanity and self-interest." Some, he feared, were trying to regain their broken fortunes in a year or two. But, on the other hand, back in Boston Edward Atkinson, textile manufacturer and member of the Educational

Committee, was delighted with the prospects. Let the rebellion be subdued this year, he said in 1863, "and the
cotton available for sale will bring more than any crop ever
brought yet." He was, in common with the Union League
clubs and the other radicals, content with the social experiment of a reconstruction which promised profits.[11]

But Abraham Lincoln had no such enthusiasm for the
social and economic experiment. When Pierce brought his
first report to Salmon Chase, the Secretary was excited,
wrote his endorsement on it, and sent Pierce along with it
to the President. Lincoln listened impatiently for only a
few minutes, then stopped the recitation. He did not think,
he said coldly, he "ought to be troubled with such details."
All he could see was that there "seemed to be an itching to
get Negroes into our lines." He sent a note along to Chase:
"I shall be obliged if the Secretary of the Treasury will in
his discretion give Mr. Pierce such instructions in regard to
Port Royal contrabands as may seem judicious."

Although Lincoln could dismiss Pierce and his contrabands frostily, he had already been troubled by details
growing out of the occupation of the Sea Islands. General
Hunter's order freeing slaves and his efforts to enlist them
into the armed forces had played a part in forcing Lincoln
to yield a little to the pressure to make the war an
Abolitionist crusade. Hunter's acts played into a growing
sentiment among Northern governors to enlist Negro
soldiers and thus avoid the necessity for drafting their
citizens into the army. Lincoln's withdrawal of Hunter's
orders brought protests from governors who wanted to use
black instead of white soldiers. Governor Richard Yates,
of Lincoln's own Illinois, told Lincoln that the "time has
come for the adoption of more decisive measures. Generals
should not be frittering away their time guarding the property of traitors, and the government ought not to spurn
the Negroes as soldiers." Iowa's Governor Samuel J.

[11] Elizabeth W. Pearson (ed.), *Letters from Port Royal* . . .
(Boston, 1906), 1-2 (Feb. 19, 1862) ; Allen Diary, 37 (Nov. 28, 1863) ;
Edward L. Pierce, *The Negroes at Port Royal* . . . (Boston, 1862),
24-25.

Kirkwood was more direct and more blunt: he wanted, he said, some "dead niggers" as well as dead white men when the war was over. If Negroes were "willing to pay for their freedom by fighting for those who make them free, I am entirely willing they should do so." Kirkwood explained that he could not "appreciate the policy that insists that all the lives lost and all the constitutions broken shall be those of white men when black men are to be found willing to do the work and take the risks." In Pennsylvania, Radical Thaddeus Stevens campaigned for re-election to Congress on the issue: "If you elect me," he promised, "I shall vote that every man be armed, black and white, who can aid in crushing the Rebellion . . . . Would it not be better that 15,000 armed slaves should lie unburied around the battlefields near Manassas than that your friends and mine should thus be there."[12]

These, however, were but protests. The actions of Governor John A. Andrew of Massachusetts, Abolitionist of the John Brown stripe, were more dangerous. When Lincoln called on the governors for more troops, Andrew replied with a declaration of "conditional patriotism." "If our people feel that they are going into the South to help fight rebels who will kill and destroy them by all the means known to savages . . . while they themselves must never 'fire at the magazine,' I think they will feel that the draft is heavy on their patriotism." But, he added, "if the President will sustain General Hunter, recognize all men, even black men, as legally capable of that loyalty the blacks are willing to manifest, and let them fight, with God and human nature on their side, the roads will swarm, if need be, with multitudes whom New England would pour out to obey your call."

But Andrew did more than make a sulky protest. Already disgusted with Lincoln, he proposed to raise no more men for "Lincoln's army." Instead, he suggested to his fellow governors of New England they should raise troops for a new army, entrust it to General Frémont who would begin

---

[12] *Demorest's New York Illustrated News*, V, 322 (Sept. 27, 1862).

a new invasion of the South. On his march, which would indeed become a gigantic John Brown raid, the advancing army should liberate and enlist Negroes who would win their own freedom. In a conference with his fellow governors at Brown University, Andrew won their support. Then he called on other governors to meet the New Englanders at Altoona, Pennsylvania. He intended to force Lincoln's hand on both Negro soldiers and emancipation, or to create a new army, under state control, which would make the war truly one "between the states."

The President learned of Andrew's plan and encouraged his own supporters among the governors to attend the Altoona meeting. Then, just as the governors assembled, Lincoln cut the ground from under them. Andrew's scheme could only rest on the humanitarian appeal of emancipation. For some time Lincoln had been contemplating the necessity of yielding to Abolitionist pressure, but cautious men among his advisers had impressed on him their fears that a proclamation of emancipation would appear to be an appeal for servile insurrection. This, of course, was precisely what Andrew proposed and what Lincoln hoped to avoid. The forthcoming meeting of the governors made action imperative.

Lincoln's advisers, and particularly Secretary William H. Seward, had pointed out that a proclamation of emancipation could only come from a government which was winning its war. Fortunately, even while the governors were participating to meet, General McClellan fought an inconclusive battle with General Robert E. Lee on Antietam Creek near Sharpsburg, Maryland. Although Lincoln never considered Sharpsburg a victory in his dealings with McClellan, it was necessary to interpret it as a victory in dealing with the threat provided by the governors. On the morning the state executives met at Altoona, the papers carried the news that Lincoln had issued his Emancipation Proclamation. The act was of dubious constitutionality and as an instrument in freeing slaves it was ineffective. It did, however, take away the basis of the radical governors' program. They were no longer able to pose as humanitarians striking a blow for human freedom while Negro soldiers fought their battles. They had forced Lincoln to yield a little, and thereafter the President was committed to add support of emancipation to his developing program of reconstruction.[13]

His acceptance, under political pressure, of emancipation did not, on the other hand, commit Lincoln to a thoroughgoing program of social reconstruction. The Emancipation Proclamation, when issued formally on New Year's Day, 1863, specifically excluded the border states still in the Union, and Virginia, Tennessee, and those parts of Louisiana in the possession of Federal troops. It applied only to areas still in Confederate hands, and over those the President had no immediate jurisdiction. Nevertheless, the excluded areas were alarmed by the potential threat to their institutions and to their property. With them Lincoln had to deal—partly to stay their fears and partly to still their opposition. His remedy, which seemed logical to him, if not to the abolition extremists, was to compensate loyal owners for their slaves. Repeatedly, he proposed to Congress, to Border State politicians, and to groups of private citizens that they support compensated emancipation. But the Border State congressmen turned him down, the visiting groups turned away silently shaking their heads, and Congress could only be brought to provide compensation for loyal owners in the District of Columbia.

Far more appealing to Lincoln than emancipation and the social experimentation of the Sea Islands was the prospect of colonizing freed Negroes outside the boundaries of the United States. Years before, men of the trustee tradition had faced the social problems of the maladjustment of the Free Negro to a white society and had formed the American Colonization Society to send Negroes back to Africa. The society was part of the general complex of associations to effect a moral regeneration of society and for long years was a better expression of the concepts of the stewards of

[13] Hesseltine, *Lincoln and the War Governors*, 254-255.

the Lord than the violent and vituperative voice of the Abolitionists. Its sponsors came from the same segment of society and it, like the other organizations, carried an economic undertone. The Republic of Liberia, which the society founded, would in the dreams of its promoters, furnish a trading post for American commerce and be the entrepôt to the riches of the African interior. In time Liberia failed to live up to its promises and the society grew weary and lost its support, but the solution it offered continued to have its appeal. Abraham Lincoln knew it was impractical. There was not enough money and shipping available, he admitted; yet, in his debates with Douglas he asserted, "my first impulse would be to free all the slaves and send them to Liberia."

The idea never lost its attractiveness. Already faced by the problem of "contrabands" who came into the Union lines and by the pressure of Sumner and the Radicals, in his first annual message Lincoln proposed an appropriation for colonizing slaves and the acquisition of suitable territory for a colony. Congress reluctantly agreed and a clause in the Confiscation Act of July 17, 1862 authorized Lincoln to make suitable arrangements with some tropical country "beyond the limits of the United States for colonizing such persons of the African race who are willing to go." In the midst of discussion various men came forward with proposals for resettling the Negroes. Frank Blair proposed setting aside a new state in Texas and James Lane of Kansas thought that it would strengthen the Mexican border. Wisconsin's James Doolittle proposed using parts of Florida; Ohio's Jacob D. Cox suggested a refuge in South Carolina and Georgia. But "some tropical country" won out, and Secretary Seward sent a circular letter to countries having likely areas. The response was varied. The Central American states, led by Costa Rica, which prided itself on being a "white man's country," declared that American Negroes would be undesirable immigrants, but Colombia and Equador agreed to accept them. Denmark had St. Croix, The Netherlands had Surinam, the British offered

Guiana. Haiti and Liberia would accept the proposed colonists.

While waiting for a suitable place, Lincoln explained his enthusiasm to a delegation of Negroes who came to see him. "Why should the people of your race be colonized, and where?" he asked rhetorically. "You and we," he answered, "are different races. We have between us a broader degree of difference than exists between almost any other two races . . . . This physical difference is a great disadvantage to us both . . . . You suffer very greatly by living among us, while we suffer from your presence." Such sentiments shocked Senator Sumner and his Radical cohorts.[14]

Out of the welter of colonization talk there came two concrete proposals. One was for a settlement at Chiriqui in Panama, the other the colonization of the Ile á Vache off the coast of Haiti. In each case there was an active promoter with a land-selling scheme; in each there was the backing of New York bankers, and in each the lush forecast of riches from exploiting the land. Chiriqui had coal deposits which the Negroes could work—and it would be, moreover, an American outpost on the potentially valuable isthmus. From adjacent Coco Island would come cotton, at least one thousand bales the first year, the promoter promised his backers. But the Chiriqui project never got under way. The shrewd promoter received $25,000 to begin operations, but the Costa Rican government protested and claimed the area and the projected colony was suspended. The Ile á Vache venture was even more unfortunate. The last day of December, 1862, the day before he issued the final and formal Emancipation Proclamation, Lincoln signed a contract with promoter Bernard Kock by which Kock would receive $50 for each Negro he settled on the island. Kock agreed to furnish the people with homes, land, food, medicines, churches, and schools, and to employ them for four years. He received $70,000 from Boston and New

[14] Nicolay and Hay, VI, 356; George R. Bently, *A History of the Freedmen's Bureau* (Philadelphia, 1955), 96-97; Charles Wesley, "Lincoln's Plans for Colonizing the Emancipated Negroes," *Journal of Negro History*, IV, 12 (Jan., 1919).

York bankers. But Lincoln and the bankers discovered that Kock was an adventurer—indeed, that he actually planned to sell his colonists to the Confederates! To protect their interests the bankers ousted Kock, took over his lease of the island, and made a fresh contract with the government. In April, 1863, 453 Negro immigrants set sail for the Haitian island. Along with them went the ebullient Kock as military governor. En route to their new home smallpox broke out among them. On arrival they found none of the promised homes and facilities. In the next few months, half-starved and abused, they lackadaisically and without tools tried to grow cotton. In October Lincoln sent an agent to investigate their conditions. He found the people hungry, mutinous (they had driven Kock out) and in trouble with the government of Haiti. They wanted to come home and the Haitian authorities wanted them to leave. Early in 1864 the government sent a vessel to evacuate them.[15]

With the failure of the Cow Island settlement Lincoln's own program of social reform had proved no more successful than the Radical-inspired experiments on the Sea Islands. Moreover, at the moment, the military governors of Tennessee and Louisiana were having difficulty in finding and organizing a loyal population that could restore their states. In fact, only Lincoln's guidance of the election in the border states and the extension of his program into Ohio and Delaware brought success. All this lay in the background when on December 8, 1863, Lincoln issued his new Proclamation of Amnesty and Reconstruction.

[15] *Ibid.*, IV, 18-19 (Jan., 1919); Paul J. Scheips, "Lincoln and the Chiriqui Colonization Project," *ibid.*, XXXVII, 418-453 (Oct., 1952); Nicolay and Hay, VI, 354-364.

CHAPTER V

The Opposing Forces: The Evolution of the Wade-Davis Bill

IN ITS FIRST IMPRESSION Lincoln's Proclamation of Amnesty and Reconstruction seemed to differ from his previous programs only in permitting Confederates to repent of their sins and pledge themselves from that time forward to lead a loyal life. Lincoln himself used the evangelical metaphor: he would, he said, hold out to sinners the opportunity for repentance. By implication, at least, he would give no countenance to Radical demands that Rebels do penance for past sins.

The immediate reaction of Republican leaders and spokesmen was favorable. Horace Greeley was completely delighted. No presidential message since George Washington's day had given "such general satisfaction." The proclamation was wise and humane, and the New York *Tribune* could not see how anyone in the South could refuse its offers. Henry Raymond's New York *Times* was in wholehearted agreement. The program of reconstruction was "simple but perfectly effective," and the closer it was examined the more it would be found "completely adapted to the great end desired." In fact, "feasibility, justice, consistency, and security" were its recommendations. The New York *Evening Post* undertook the closer examination and emerged with the glowing conclusion that "it would be almost ludicrous pedantry to criticize the President's message." The political problem, explained the *Post*, was the most difficult ever posed a statesman. Lincoln had avoided the extreme of declaring the rebellious states mere territories, and the extreme of merely telling the Rebels that, if they laid down their arms, they would be restored to full communion with their fellow citizens. The President had been magnanimous and lenient. He offered the Rebels, not only a peace that saved them from the miseries of war, but also an "honorable pardon." And the President's secretaries, John Nicolay and John Hay, watching carefully for congressional reactions, long afterward remembered that "men acted as though the millenium had come." Zachariah Chandler was delighted; Charles Sumner "forgot for the moment his doctrine of state suicide."[1]

It was the Democratic press, ever skeptical of Lincoln and hostile to the Radical Republicans, that found the proclamation dubious. It was, said the New York *World*, a "creditable speciment of political dexterity," falling—even as the *Post* declared it to be—between the extreme Radical and the moderate Republican positions. For the Radicals Lincoln promised not to modify the drive for emancipation, and for the conservatives he promised not to disturb any arrangements of the state governments for taking care of the Negroes. But, said the *World*, the scheme was preposterous. The states would be pyramids resting on an apex of 10 per cent of their citizens. The oath would erect a minority into a privileged class with all political power. The Democratic New York *Herald* merely scoffed at the 10 per cent plan, thinking there were not "that many good men there." Each of the opposition papers perceived the political aspects of the proclamation. It was "a party manifesto," said the *World*, and "looked toward the nominating convention in the summer and the presidential election in the

[1] New York *Evening Post*, Dec. 10, New York *Tribune*, New York *Times*, Dec. 11, 1863. Nicolay and Hay, IX, 109. Noah Brooks wrote that he saw Sumner listening to the message with "undistinguished impatience." He "withdrew his attention, . . . and in a boyish and petulant manner slammed his books and documents about his desk and upon the floor, and generally exhibited his ill temper to an astonished and admiring gallery" (*Washington in Lincoln's Time*, ed. by Herbert Mitgang [New York, 1959], 151).

fall." By setting up state governments representing one-
tenth of the voters, stated the *World* bluntly, "he can control
as many electoral votes as may be needed to turn the scale."[2]
Soon, other Democratic papers began to lay before their
readers tables of votes under Lincoln's 10 per cent plan
of reconstruction.[3]

It remained, however, for Horatio Seymour, Democratic
governor of New York and one of the ablest minds in the
Democratic party, to undertake a careful analysis of the
political implications of the proclamation and to set it
against its background. Seymour had had his troubles with
the administration. He had a firm belief in the rights of
the states and the limited powers of the Federal government, and he had opposed the many-fronted drive towards
nationalization and centralization. He favored compromise,
adjustments with the South, and the restoration of the old
Union. He saw, more clearly than most, that the war was

---

[2] James G. Randall and Richard N. Current, *Lincoln the President* . . .
(New York, 1958), IV, 8; New York *World*, Dec. 10, 1863.

[3] Under the heading, "The One-Tenth Vote," the Detroit *Free Press*,
Dec. 24, 1863, stated:
"The following table is of interest as showing the vote cast for
President in 1860, and the number required to be polled to justify
the readmission of the rebel states under the President's Amnesty
Proclamation.

States	Total Votes in 1860	No. Required
Alabama	90,857	9,086
Arkansas	54,053	5,406
Florida	14,247	1,435
Georgia	106,365	10,637
Louisiana	50,500	5,050
Mississippi	69,120	6,912
Tennessee	145,333	14,334
North Carolina	96,230	9,623
Texas	62,986	6,298

"Virginia and South Carolina are not included in the list because
the former is not mentioned in the proclamation and the latter never
casts presidential votes. No doubt an effort will soon be made to
reorganize the state governments in Louisiana, Arkansas, and
Tennessee, and as Military Governors are not particular, in case
there are not sufficient number of bona fide votes, enough loyal
soldiers can be supplied to make up the deficiency. It ought to be
an easy matter to raise 4,000 loyal votes in Louisiana, 5,000 in
Arkansas, and 15,000 in Tennessee. If Mobile should be captured
during the present winter, enough of Mississippi might fall into our
possession to include 7,000 loyal voters, and if General Banks keeps
ahead at his present rate, Texas with 6,000 voters is not an im-
possibility before the coming summer."

creating an imbalance of economic power in the Union, and threatening to make the New England region dominant in the nation. He was opposed to emancipation and to conscription. In the summer of 1863, when he presented evidence that the draft quotas assigned to New York were so adjusted as to bear heaviest on the Democratic districts, he won his case and forced the War Department to establish just quotas. His victory, however, was hidden by the furor over the Draft Riots of July, 1863. He was, moreover, personally indignant at the insinuations and open charges emanating from high Republican circles in Washington that he was a "copperhead," a "Peace Democrat," and a secret ally of Jefferson Davis. Horatio Seymour was in no mood to accept unquestioningly any proclamation bearing the external evidence of leniency and magnanimity that came from Abraham Lincoln. On January 5, 1864 he presented his analysis of Lincoln's plan of reconstruction in his annual message to the New York legislature.

First, he had something to say about conscription. It was, he explained carefully, a means of destroying the power of the state over its citizens. It would make an army of conscripts, estranged from the people, and a peril to the Republic. Such an army could make a president. With such an army, a president could make himself a dictator.

As for the proposed program of reconstruction, Seymour saw it as a new drive to destroy the South. The plan called for the continued maintenance of an army with a continuous drain upon the persons and property of the people. Whenever one-tenth of the voters submitted to the humiliation of taking an oath to support all future presidential proclamations on slavery, they might form new governments. This minority would be kept in power by the arms and treasure of the North. There would be, explained Seymour with a keen eye to the political realities, no motive to bring the rest of the population into the government. Instead, "there will be every inducement of power, of gain, and of ambition, to perpetuate the condition." At the same time, it would be to the interest of the national administration to

continue this system of government. And the state governments so formed would represent the power creating them.

Repeating the figures which the Democratic press had
been parading, the indignant Governor pointed out that nine
states controlled by Lincoln would balance in the electoral
college, in the Senate and in the House, the states of New
York, Pennsylvania, Illinois, Indiana, Massachusetts, Missouri, Kentucky, and Wisconsin—of 16,533,383 people,
which was equal to or greater than one-half of the country.
In Florida, 1,400 men would balance in the Senate the power
of New York. Seventy thousand in the South could weigh
down the nine most populous states of the North. Together
with Virginia and West Virginia, there would be a system
of rotten boroughs which would govern the Union, destroy
the representative nature of the government, and enable an
administration to perpetuate itself in power.

It was significant, Seymour added, that every measure
to convert the war into a war against personal liberty and
property in the South had been accompanied by claims to
exercise military power in the North. The Emancipation
Proclamation had been paralleled by the suspension of
habeas corpus, the confiscation acts by arbitrary arrests,
the plan of reconstruction by armed interference in local
elections. Each act was proclaimed as necessary for winning
the war—but, said the Governor with either a lack of complete candor or a highly optimistic view of the military
situation, "more prerogatives are asserted in the hour of
triumph than were claimed as a necessity in days of
disaster." The President's plan, as Governor Seymour
analyzed it, was a measure for fastening military despotism
over one-third of the country, and would be the basis for extending an armed dictatorship over the whole land.[4]

Radicals in Congress did not need Seymour's able analysis
and exposition to alert them to the political implications of
Lincoln's proclamation. Almost immediately they recovered
from whatever initial enthusiasm they might have had, and

---

[4] *Annual Message of the Governor of the State of New York, January
5, 1864* (Albany, 1864), 55-57.

began to voice their opposition. The politically-minded among them found the forthcoming national convention and election as the reasons back of Lincoln's scheme. As clearly as any Democrat they perceived the strength that the President's "rotten boroughs" would give him. At the same time the social reformers and economic exploiters in Congress saw no hopes in states that could be tightly controlled by a president who had no sympathy with their views and who had the army to back him. Each for his own reason launched criticism at the President. "Abraham's proclamation, take it altogether," said Maine's W. P. Fessenden, "was a silly performance. Think of telling the rebels they may fight as long as they can, and take a pardon when they have had enough." Quickly the opponents hit upon the plan's patent weakness—its lack of democracy! It was a "mockery of democratic principles," explained old Thaddeus Stevens, who was advocating reducing the "conquered provinces" of the South to territories and permitting no exercise of political rights. It violates "American principles," said Ohio's Ben Wade, who declared that "until majorities can be found loyal and trustworthy for state government, they must be governed by a stronger hand."[5]

Whatever inconsistencies there may have been in the Radicals' exposition of American principles of democracy, they were on sounder ground when they rested their case on the Constitution. The determination of the exact time when a state government met the constitutional requirement that it be republican in form rested in Congress. "The executive ought not to be permitted to handle this great question to his own liking," intoned Wade. The President was exceeding his constitutional power, said Sumner. It was the duty of Congress to see that no Rebel state was prematurely restored. Proper safeguards must be established. In the House the whole matter of slavery and reconstruction was

[5] T. Harry Williams, *Lincoln and the Radicals* (Madison, 1941), 302, 320; Richard N. Current, *Old Thad Stevens* (Madison, 1942), 189; *Congressional Globe*, 38 Cong. 1 Sess., XXXIV (1), 5, 523 (Dec. 7, 1863; Feb. 8, 1864), hereinafter *CG*.

referred to a special committee under the chairmanship of Maryland's Henry Winter Davis.

While congressmen formed their lines against the President, events in the occupied areas of the South began to test both the form and the substance of Lincoln's plan of reconstruction. In two states, Louisiana and Tennessee, where the military governors were laboring to establish governments on the basis of the loyalist population, Lincoln's new offer of amnesty to Confederates brought confusion into the already divided ranks of the Unionists.

In Tennessee the processes of reconstruction were already slow. Andrew Johnson had shown no haste in holding elections but had waited for a Union party to get organized. In September Lincoln had prodded him and Johnson, who showed more aptitude for speechmaking than for administration, had explained to a mass meeting in Nashville that Tennessee was not out of the Union, and that "one by one" all the agencies of the state government would be set in motion. A legislature would be elected, temporary judges appointed, interim sheriffs take over. "There is nothing in the way but obstinacy," he said.[6]

Yet it seemed, indeed, that it was Johnson's own obstinacy that stood in the way. Neither Johnson nor the Unionists he was slowly rallying was eager to extend amnesty to Confederates. In Memphis the editor of the *Bulletin* was more concerned with purging the Unionist ranks of non-emancipationists than he was in getting a government established. In the summer of 1862 a mayor and board of aldermen were chosen and Editor J. B. Bingham was convinced that "the grossest frauds" had occurred in the election. The ticket of the "unconditional Union men, composed of gentlemen," went down to defeat, and "the most dissolute and unworthy men in the community placed in office." They were, in his opinion, "ignorant and unprincipled men, of low instincts, without honor or social position" and intent upon corruption. He wanted Johnson

[6] *Appleton's Cyclopaedia* . . . (New York, 1864-1870), III, 828 (hereinafter AP).

to remove them. Nor was Johnson eager to extend the suffrage to other than "unconditional" Union men. In January he arranged a large rally to call for a constitutional convention. To the rally he urged that only loyal men be rewarded and that "repentant sinners" be made to "do penance." Civil government should be instituted only by loyal citizens. He called for an election for county offices and for a constitutional convention in March, but he announced that "it is not expected that the enemies of the United States will propose to vote, nor is it intended that they be permitted to vote or hold office." Early in February Horace G. Maynard, Unionist who had refused to withdraw from Congress when Tennessee seceded and was now acting as Johnson's attorney general, announced that the disloyal people had lost their citizenship and could not vote until six months after they had taken the oath.

Lincoln himself tried persuasion on Johnson and the Tennessee Unionists who were bent on proscription. Loyal people as well as the formerly disloyal should, he advised, take the oath. "It does not hurt them, clears all question of their right to vote, and swells the aggregate number of those who take it, which is an important object." But Unionists, who thought their sufferings bore ample testimony to their loyalty, resented being classed with the former disloyal people. Then too, many of the loyalists objected to taking an oath which committed them to support all future proclamations against slavery, and many who had opposed secession were equally opposed to emancipation and Negro equality. But these were the very men whom Johnson and the "unconditional Unionists" wanted to purge. Governor Johnson formulated a new oath which committed the emotions as well as the acts of its takers: "I ardently desire," it read, "the suppression of the present insurrection . . . the success of its armies, and the defeat of all those who oppose them . . . and all laws and proclamations . . . may be speedily and permanently established and enforced over all the people, states, and territories . . . ." Fully trusting Johnson, Lincoln accepted the substitute, but

Johnson's enemies promptly dubbed the new pledge the "Damnesty Oath."[7]

Amid confusion and squabbles which were dividing "conservatives" from "unconditional Unionists" in Tennessee, came the March election. The "new citizens" did not vote, but soldiers and government employees, who had been stationed in a county for six months, went to the polls. In places where the Federal soldiers and officeholders were stationed, unconditional Unionists won. In other counties, mere Unionists, dubbed conservatives, took the offices. The result was thoroughly disappointing to Johnson and he delayed still further implementing the formation of a state government.

In the meantime, however, the Union League was active in organizing the unconditional Unionist forces. Before the Republicans met in nominating convention in Baltimore, Unionist meetings had endorsed Lincoln for president and sent a delegation to Baltimore pledged to support Johnson for the vice-presidency.

In Louisiana, the other state where the military government was already in the process of making a civil government when Lincoln issued his proclamation, the immediate impact of the new program was less confusing than in Tennessee. There it seemed that everything was going smoothly. In January General N. P. Banks set Washington's birthday as election day for six executive officers of the state and provided that they should take office on March 4, 1864. In April he would hold an election for a convention to revise the Constitution. In two months, promised the New York *Times*, January 21, 1864, as it reported Banks's actions, Louisiana would be as completely loyal as New York, and in three months it would be free of slavery. "The loyal sentiment of the state is now almost identical with the anti-slavery sentiment."[8]

But this, indeed, was a source of trouble. The loyalist

[7] Hall, 118-120; *ORA*, 3, IV, 46; Vernon M. Queener, "The Origin of the Republican Party in East Tennessee," *ETHSP*, XX, 79 (1948).
[8] Hall, 122.

groups, not yet purged of pro-slavery elements by Butler and Banks, were organizing. To them Lincoln's amnesty proclamation might add others who could accept emancipation and repent secession, but who were hardly likely to subscribe to the social and economic program which had become identified with radical anti-slavery sentiment. At the same time, pro-slavery loyalists objected to making a blanket pledge to support all future emancipation measures. Late in January Banks appealed to Lincoln to clarify matters. There were Unionists who did not want to take the oath, others who thought it not strong enough. Lincoln refused to be committed. He had carefully provided, he pointed out, the course to be followed. In his message to Congress he had declared: "Saying that reconstruction will be accepted if presented in a specified way, it is not to be said it will never be accepted in any other way." So, he added, "you are at liberty to adopt any rule which shall admit to vote any unquestionably loyal free-state men and none others." And yet, he sighed, "I do wish they would all take the oath."

Given a free hand, Banks added clarification in a proclamation which defined who might take the oath. Every white male, a citizen of the United States, resident in Louisiana for a year and of his parish for six months, who took the oath could vote. Citizens expelled from their homes by Rebels could vote where they resided, and Louisianans in the Federal army could vote wherever they were. The presidential pardon, explained Banks, applied "only to those who have committed treason." To others the oath was merely a pledge of continued fealty to the government. But as Banks made abundantly clear, indifference to setting up the new government—that is, failure to participate— would be regarded as a crime. Under this clarification, 9,995 voters registered, of whom 4,000 had not been naturalized, and 4,910 "unperfectly" qualified. On Washington's birthday 5,000 of these voters chose Michael Hahn to be governor.[9]

[9] Basler, VII, 161-162; Caskey, 102ff.

On March 6 Banks—assisted by Military Governor Shepley, who had taken no active part in creating the new government—inaugurated Governor Hahn. Lincoln promptly wired his congratulations to the "first free state governor of Louisiana," and Banks turned over the state treasury of $381,000 Federal greenbacks and $460,000 Confederate notes to the new executive. Five days later Banks ordered an election for a constitutional convention on the same terms and with the same election officials as in the gubernatorial election. It was less than a month from the beginning of the Hahn government but already charges of fraud and of army interference marred the harmony of the election. A congressional investigation later reported that the whole "scheme in Louisiana has been a complete failure, and is regarded by the loyal people of the state as a vast scheme of fraud enforced by military rule by which a few political tricksters have taken the reins of government into their own hands for their especial benefit and emolument and in direct opposition to the popular will." It was the investigators' opinion that, if the provisions of the President's proclamation had been adhered to, "the number of votes polled would have been much less than 10 per cent." Nevertheless, early in April 150 duly elected delegates assembled in New Orleans to debate changes in the constitution. The reconstruction of Louisiana was proceeding apace.

To Governor Hahn on the eve of the convention Lincoln sent a plea—designed to forestall the mounting Radical drive for Negro suffrage—to admit a few colored people to the vote. Just, he suggested, "the very intelligent, and especially those who have fought gallantly in our ranks." The convention, however, refused to accept even a limited Negro suffrage and only reluctantly provided that Negro schools might receive state support. Whatever else the reconstructing government of Louisiana displayed, it made clear that it was not prepared to follow Lincoln's leadership. The Unionists of Louisiana, however, sent a solid Lincoln delegation to the Baltimore convention of the "Union Party."[10]

[10] *Ibid.*, 118-119; Basler, VII, 243.

Perhaps, indeed, neither Louisiana nor Tennessee furnished a fair test of Lincoln's plan of amnesty and reconstruction. In both states the process of reconstruction under military governments was under way when the President issued his proclamation. Lincoln hoped, however, that other Southern states might be restored by his plan, and early in January, 1864 he sent agents, armed with blank books for oath-takers to sign, to Arkansas and Florida. He had hopes, as well, for Texas.

In Arkansas, where Lincoln had prematurely appointed John S. Phelps as military governor in the spring of 1862, there was now General Frederick Steele, commanding at Little Rock and exercising control over the civilian population. On January 5, 1864 Lincoln sent General Nathan Kimball to Arkansas with an armload of blank books for enrolling oath-takers. Earlier the commander at Memphis had sent Kimball to Lincoln to assure the President that Arkansas could be reconstructed with the same kind of "Unconditional Union" men that were proving effective in Memphis. "I desire," Lincoln told Steele as he sent Kimball back, "to afford the people of Arkansas an opportunity of taking the oath." Detail officers, he ordered, to start administering the oath to loyal and repentant men. Two weeks later Lincoln had more information and more instructions. "Sundry citizens," he said, petitioned for an election for state officers and for a constitutional convention which would abolish slavery. The President set March 28 as election day and ordered the voters attending the polling places at eight o'clock that morning should choose judges and clerks of the election—and then, or before, the voters should take the oath prescribed. There must be, added the President, a minimum of 5,406 votes.[11]

This was more direct intervention and more personal control than Lincoln was displaying in other places. In Tennessee and Louisiana he was allowing the governors to add punitive features to the process of becoming loyal,

[11] Nicolay and Hay, VII, 277-278; *AP*, III, 16.

and the Unionist convention in Nashville was resolving that oath-taking Confederates be proscribed. In these states, too, the military governors were appointing election officials. But in Arkansas the President himself was prescribing the basic procedures.

If Lincoln was seeking to avoid in Arkansas the quarrels that were developing in Tennessee and Louisiana, he was moving too late. Before Kimball could arrive with his oath books, a convention of the Unconditional Unionists had assembled in Little Rock. The 45 delegates claimed to represent 23 of the state's 57 counties, but 10 of the 23 were still completely or largely in Confederate hands. The convention quickly abolished slavery—with one dissenting vote—and defined the qualifications for the suffrage to conform with Lincoln's proclamation. On the eve of the convention Steele's soldiers arrested the editor and stopped the presses of the Little Rock *Democrat*. A new paper, announced the military, would be started by men of undoubted loyalty, who would use their influence for reorganizing civil government in the state. The convention approved the act and proceeded to install a provisional governor, lieutenant-governor, and secretary of state.

The haste in these proceedings gave Lincoln qualms. He did not, however, want to overthrow the home-grown movement, and he instructed Steele to coöperate with the provisional government. "Be sure to retain the free state constitutional provisions," he advised, "and you can fix the rest." In a follow-up telegram he urged, "Of all things avoid if possible a dividing into cliques among the friends of the common objectives."[12]

For a moment Lincoln thought of sending General Daniel E. Sickles to Arkansas and New Orleans to report on the progress of reconstruction—"how the amnesty proclamation works, if at all"—and "whether deserters come in from the enemy." But Arkansas' Governor Phelps hurriedly pleaded with Lincoln not to send Sickles and assured him that

[12] Nicolay and Hay, VII, 296-299; New York *Times*, Jan. 26, 1864.

General Steele had everything in hand. Lincoln accepted the assurance and, when opponents of Steele's arrangements carried their bickerings to the White House, Lincoln merely referred them to Steele. "Some single mind must be the master," he explained—and Steele was on the ground. Actually, Steele showed energy and the desired single-mindedness. He set an election day, solemnly promised there would be "no interference from any quarter" with the "free expression of the loyal men of the state on that day." The election went off quietly. The soldiers voted in their camps and citizens from distant counties, who were in Little Rock, cast their votes for their counties' officers. The candidates elected to county offices and to the legislature came largely from the Arkansas regiment in the Federal army. But this, explained the New York *Times* as it recounted the steady progress of reconstruction in Arkansas, was to be expected. "But few really sound men were to be found" outside the troops. And Lincoln was pleased. More than the requisite one-tenth had voted. "I am much gratified that you got out so large a vote, so nearly all the right way." He was pleased, too, that the legislature organized and got quickly into "working order." "Whatever I can I will do to protect you," he promised.[13]

The relative success in Arkansas had no parallel in Florida. In the middle of January, just after he sent the blank books to Arkansas, Lincoln dispatched John Hay, his private secretary, bolstered with a commission as a major, to General Q. A. Gilmore in South Carolina. Hay told Gilmore that he understood that an effort was "being made by some worthy men in Florida" to reconstruct a legal state government. Late in the month Gilmore issued a proclamation, calling attention to Lincoln's proclamation and to Hay's presence with blank books. Hay would be at Fernandina to extend to citizens an opportunity to take the oath. Optimistically, Gilmore reported to Lincoln that the

[13] Basler, VII, 185; *AP*, IV, 29; New York *Times*, Apr. 12, New York *World*, Feb. 15, 1864.

plan being followed by Banks in Louisiana could be dupli-
cated in Florida.

The Florida scheme depended on the success of a military
expedition, and neither the military nor the political adven-
ture went well. The army moved toward the St. John's
River, expecting to bring out cotton. The move had little
support in the War Department. Secretary Stanton left
the matter up to Halleck. Perhaps, he said, if cotton came
out and Negroes enlisted in sufficient numbers, the expedition might be justified, "but simply as a military
operation, I attach very little importance to such expenditures." The New York *Times*, reporting on the plans,
confessed it could see "no adequate object" in the venture.
But the *World*, ever alert to the political implications of the
administration's moves, instructed its rival. "Have we not
a new President to elect, oh simple heart?" it asked. "And
has not President Lincoln declared his willingness to receive
and enjoy in the coming presidential election one-tenth of
the former vote, just as much as if it were the ten-tenths?
And oh, naive and wondering politicians, is not Florida a
very thinly populated state, and will not a very slight
expeditionary force, all voters, amount to the one, and
greatly desired, tenth?" But John Hay could not even
get the 1,400 signers who would be sufficient by Lincoln's
proclamation, to reconstruct the state.[14]

Whatever the validity of the *World's* analysis of the
Florida expedition, the coincidence of political moves seemed
to lend credibility to Democratic skepticism. Just as the
Florida affair was getting into the papers and events were
maturing in Arkansas, Louisiana, and Tennessee, Lincoln's
supporters took steps to insure his renomination. Near the
middle of February a circular addressed to "loyal people
everywhere" without regard to party, appeared. It was
signed by Samuel Draper, stockbroker, and by two dozen
leading businessmen of New York, and advised all men

[14] *ORA*, 1, I, XXXV, 294-295; New York *Times*, Apr. 12, New York
World, Feb. 15, 1864.

desiring Lincoln's re-election to assemble in their localities on Washington's birthday to endorse the administration. And at the same time Montgomery Blair, with the patronage of the Post Office Department behind him, was working on the state legislatures. On the appointed day mass meetings and legislatures duly passed the desired resolutions. Among them were endorsements from Nashville and from the voters assembled that day in New Orleans. It was clearly a move to influence the Baltimore convention, and it forestalled any Radical efforts to organize behind another standard-bearer.[15]

Radical hopes, in fact, of preventing Lincoln's renomination were fading everywhere in the spring of 1864. The premature publication of Senator S. C. Pomeroy's circular boosting Secretary Chase played into Lincoln's hand, and no other candidate emerged with any show of strength. There was some talk of Frémont, even about Ben Butler, but when the Republicans gathered in the Union Party convention, only Missouri's delegation was off the Lincoln bandwagon. The Missourians' forlorn hope was General Grant. Lincoln's use of the patronage, his control of the army, and the clear demonstration of the elections of 1863 that he could and would use the army at the polls gave him full support at the convention. He did not need the delegations, which were duly recognized and seated, from the two Virginias, Tennessee, and Louisiana.

Although they could not prevent his renomination, the Radicals were determined to prevent Lincoln from controlling the processes of reconstruction. Fully conscious of the Democratic charges about pocket boroughs and the imminence of military dictatorship, they were determined to prevent executive control. Intent upon punishing the Rebels and reordering the social and economic order of the South, they hurriedly searched for a different plan of reconstruction.

While Henry Winter Davis' committee in the House of

[15] Richard Yates Papers, Jan. 28, 1864 (Illinois State Historical Library, Springfield); *Missouri Democrat* (St. Louis), Feb. 12, 1864.

Representatives pondered various schemes, the Radicals on the floors of the House and Senate and the propaganda societies of the eastern cities made amply clear their continuing animosity to the South and their determination to permit no simple and easy restoration of the old Union. In the Senate Sumner worked steadily, and before the close of the session he had the satisfaction of seeing the Fugitive Slave Act of 1850 repealed and a Thirteenth Amendment abolishing slavery going out to the state legislatures for ratification. In the meantime he was reiterating the dogma that reconstruction was the exclusive prerogative of Congress. In December, less than a week after Lincoln's proclamation, Sumner was willing to dismiss it as unimportant. Any plan which guaranteed emancipation, he told James Bright in England, "will suit me." He doubted "if the details will be remembered a fortnight from now." But in the fortnight Lincoln's pressures on Tennessee and Louisiana were bringing action, and Sumner began to pay attention to the details. In February he offered resolutions "so that . . . every star in our national flag shall represent a state . . . care must be taken that the rebellion is not allowed, through any negligence or mistaken concession, to retain the least foothold for future activity." The care would have to be taken by Congress. In May he was insisting that any state "pretending to secede" be "regarded as a rebel state," subject to military occupation, and only to be readmitted by joint action of the two houses of Congress. But by that time Winter Davis' bill from the House was before the Senate.[16]

While Sumner, ably assisted by his fellow Radicals, was keeping the Senate aware of the evil implications of Lincoln's plan, Henry Winter Davis' committee was fumbling for an alternative scheme. In February there came an indication that the House Radicals would not weaken before Lincoln's pressure. Knocking on the door of the House came Colonel James M. Johnson, officer of a Union regi-

[16] New York *World*, Feb. 12, 1864; *CG*, 38 Cong., 1 Sess., XXXIV (2), 536-538, 1481-1491 (Feb. 9, Apr. 8, 1864).

ment, bearing credentials signed by General Steele, certifying him to be a newly-elected congressman from Arkansas. Promptly, Davis questioned the credentials. The Congress did not know that a state government existed in Arkansas. From Massachusetts' George Boutwell came an echo: Arkansas had no legal existence as a state. "When," asked a Democrat from New York, "did the states cease to exist?" Carefully—patronizingly—Boutwell explained: "A state exists by the will of its people. Arkansas can exist again by the will of its people, and not with military force and coercion in the arrangement of its state government." Clearly, the Radicals did not intend to accept an army-created 10 per cent as constituting the people of a state. The President's proclamation, said Davis, was "a grave usurpation upon the legislative authority of the people." Lincoln, he explained, had "called on General Banks to organize another hermaphrodite government, half military, half republican, representing the alligators and frogs of Louisiana" and had placed it on an equality with states of the United States.[17]

Late in January Henry Winter Davis had a bill ready to report, but the House rejected his motion to put it on the calendar. The Marylander was not popular with his fellows and they yielded only reluctantly to his wishes. It was the middle of February before he could get authorization to print his bill, and not until March 22 did it come up for discussion. The bill spelled out the steps in the reconstruction of a state. First of all, it provided that no step was to be taken until all armed resistance to the Federal authority had ceased in the rebellious states. Then the President should appoint a provisional governor (but not necessarily a military man), who would have the pay and emoluments of a brigadier general. The governor should administer the government and enforce all the laws of the United States and of the state—as of 1860—except for the laws supporting slavery in the state. He should collect the taxes provided in the laws of 1860, make expenditures neces-

[17] *Ibid.*, 38 Cong., 1 Sess., XXXIV (1), 682 (Feb. 16, 1864).

sary, and turn the residue of the revenue over to the Federal treasury. The governor should enroll all white male citizens, and should offer to all, except Confederate officers and soldiers, the opportunity of taking the oath of allegiance as prescribed by an act of Congress of July 2, 1862. When one-tenth of the enrolled citizens had taken the oath, he should order elections for a state convention. The convention should contain a number equal to the two houses of the state legislature in 1860, but the governor should assign the number of delegates to the districts. The convention, when assembled, should frame a new constitution for the state which would contain provisions excluding Confederate and state officials—except those whose duties were purely ministerial—should abolish slavery, and should repudiate the Rebel debt of the state. When this constitution had been approved by the voters, the governor might order elections under the rules prescribed by the convention, and when the final result was approved by Congress it might authorize the President to issue a proclamation declaring the state restored to the Union.[18]

The difference between the Davis bill and the President's proclamation was not so extensive as appeared on the surface. The latter excluded from amnesty the higher ranking officers of the Confederate government and army, while the former excluded them primarily from the initial stages of reconstruction. The bill contemplated provisional governors and spelled out their powers, but they were not essentially different from the orders which Lincoln and the War Department had issued to the military governors. More fundamental were two implications of the bill: in the first place, its action was delayed until the rebellion had disappeared, and in the second place it prescribed a complicated procedure for the restoration of the state. There were seven steps in the congressional proposal—five more than in Lincoln's device—and at each step Congress by regulation or acceptance could control the process. It

[18] Nicolay and Hay, IX, 109-119; *CG,* 38 Cong., 1 Sess., XXXIV (1), 278-280 (Jan. 20, 1864).

was, however, neither well thought out nor strongly held. It was less a process of reconstruction than a device for striking at the President's power.

The discussion of the bill brought out a multiplicity of views regarding the South, slavery, Lincoln's plan of reconstruction, and the constitutional status of the rebellious states. The speakers who addressed themselves to the subject, however, seldom bothered to give attention to the bill itself. The propositions that came from the committee excited no interest: members refrained from analyzing the bill item by item and from proposing pertinent amendments. Few members discussed the ultimate objectives of reconstruction or had constructive suggestions to make to advance social or economic ends. The debate, moreover, excited little interest among the leading lights on the Republican side of the House. The situation, however, received ample airing, and it had attention, not only in the specific discussion on the Davis bill, but also in the committee of the whole when constitutional amendments, military interference in elections, and even revenue measures were the proper subjects of debate.

When the discussion opened, Davis and other Radical members of his committee hastened to forestall one objection. Between the time the bill was printed and its discussion, the Committee had determined to abandon the 10 per cent provision it had picked up from Lincoln's proclamation and to require that a majority of the enrolled citizens in a state must take the oath of allegiance. The lateness of the change from one-tenth to one-half the citizens may have indicated that no one considered the 40 per cent difference between the two schemes as a matter of vital importance. The members directed their attention to other things.

Davis began the formal discussion of his bill with an extensive argument that the bill rested on the constitutional provision that Congress should guarantee to every state a republican form of government. He insisted that it was the duty of the Congress and not the executive to make this guarantee. From this, he launched into a Radical exposition of the view that slavery was incompatible with a republican form of government. His bill was, he explained, a means of ridding the country of slavery. Lincoln's Emancipation Proclamation, of dubious validity, had not ended slavery in loyal territories. The President's reconstruction governments might indeed end slavery in the states where they operated, but they did not prevent slaveholders from selling their chattel to other places where slavery was protected. His program of reconstruction would eliminate slavery or would, at least, be a step in that direction.

Few of the members who discussed the bill paid attention to the anti-slavery argument. They were, in fact, more interested in discussing the President's proclamation and the nature of executive usurpation. Lincoln, said Indiana's Henry W. Harrington, made treason the foundation of reconstruction, the main pillar of universal liberty. Men who had been three years in arms against the United States could have forgiveness "provided only that they are content to be the slavish instruments of Mr. Lincoln." They were to be "warders of the inner temple, and the equals of their recent slaves." The basis of representative government was that the majority should control. But Lincoln had "discovered . . . that an oath of fealty to himself is equal to the votes of nine men and the act of taking the oath and voting gives a plain constitutional majority."

James C. Allen, representative from Illinois, apologized to the House for mentioning Lincoln's proclamation, because "it may be deemed a work of supererogation to discuss a document of such unlimited pretention that has so soon fallen into such general contempt." It was intended to increase the President's power in Congress and in the electoral college. It was, echoed New Jersey's Nehemiah Perry, designed to get a majority of the delegates to the nominating convention—a "political trick worthy of the most adroit and unscrupulous wire puller." And S. S. "Sunset" Cox of Ohio turned once more to spelling out the significance of one-tenth of the 679,310 voters of nine states in 1860 which were now represented by 67,931. It was a "mockery" to call 14,534 voters of Tennessee the equivalent of ten times their number, "but it will do to make him a candidate, and more than that, it might elect him president."

The Republicans allowed the Democrats to attack the President and to point out the despotic features of his plan of reconstruction. When they came to speak on the bill or on related subjects, they signalized their agreement with the Democrats with softer words. They were sure that General Banks's government in Louisiana was worthless, that the Arkansas experiment was disastrous. Davis, indeed, agreed that Lincoln's proclamation was not worth the paper it was written on; George Boutwell agreed that the country should avoid the exercise of military authority. No one, in fact, had a word of defense to offer for Lincoln.

On the other hand, there were few words of enthusiasm uttered for Davis' bill. Boutwell endorsed the bill but devoted much of his time to pointing out the areas of his disagreement. He would not, for example, have limited the suffrage to whites and he thought that the limitation of the bill—and of Lincoln's proclamation as well—to the existing boundaries and names of the states was evil. He would have preferred to have the names of South Carolina and Georgia never again appear in the list of states. He thought it would be better to turn South Carolina, Georgia, and Florida over to the freedmen—setting them aside for the Negroes in perpetuity. Delaware's Nathaniel B. Smithers, on the other hand, made an able defense and exposition of the bill. He explained its terms, dully enough, and turned with more enthusiasm to justifying the measure. He was sure that Congress must guarantee the republican form of government in the states. He met the objections that the bill did not rest, in true democratic tradition, upon the consent of the governed. "I deny that a rebel has any political rights," he asserted. Therefore, the government needed only to rest on the consent of the loyal. As for the argument advanced by the Democrats against both the bill and Lincoln's proclamation that the rights of the states were being destroyed, he raised an indignant voice. "Mr. Speaker, it is time that there was an end to this delusion. The danger to this people is not from centralization but disintegration . . . . Homogeneity of institutions is our only safeguard, universal freedom the only possible solution."

It was May 4 before the bill came to a vote in the House. By a parliamentary squabble, the preamble was voted down and there was a momentary chance the bill would be lost. The attendance was at a minimum, but finally it passed by a none too impressive majority—73 to 59.

In the Senate the bill went to the Committee on Territories, whose chairman was Benjamin F. Wade of Ohio. Late in the month he reported that his committee was ready to bring up the bill, but got no permission to introduce it. It was June 29, but five days before the end of the session, before he could get a hearing and then the Senate voted 17 to 11 against discussing it.   On July 1 he succeeded in getting it before the Senate.

It was, said Wade in presenting the measure, an important bill.   The executive ought not to be permitted to handle this great question to his own liking.   His proclamation was not based on the fundamental principle of Americanism.   Forgetting that Davis and his committee had originally been uncritical of the 10 per cent figure, Wade launched an assault on Lincoln's violation of the basic principle of majority rule.   John S. Carlile of West Virginia agreed in the assault on Lincoln, but he added that Congress itself did not possess the power to control a state.   The bill was revolutionary; no state had a republican form of government, when its government was prescribed by an outside power.

There was clearly no interest in the Senate in the bill. B. Gratz Brown of Missouri, Radical opponent of Lincoln, cut to the heart of the measure with an amendment.   He proposed that everything after the preamble be omitted in favor of a substitute statement that states in rebellion could not cast a vote for electors or for senators and representatives until the insurrection was suppressed and the people had returned to their obedience. A later act of Congress would determine when that had happened. The Brown amendment dealt precisely with the only issue—the use of the states in the election. The hour was late and Washington's heat was oppressive. "Sitting in this furnace beneath this heat," Brown demanded a vote. His amendment carried by one vote—17 to 16, with 16 absentees recorded. Senator Sumner offered to add a further amendment enacting the emancipation proclamation. But this non-germane proposition met a deserved fate. The Senate rejected it by 21 to 11.

Back in the House, in the last day of the session, Davis made a desperate and apparently hopeless effort to save his bill. He moved that the House not concur in the Senate's amendment and appoint a conference committee. Thaddeus Stevens advised against it. Accept the Senate substitute, he urged. He did not want to see Arkansas' electors counted in the election. But Davis thought they should confer—if only to see if they could get something better. Vote after vote failed because of no quorum. Finally, the tellers rounded a bare quorum from the sweltering anterooms and the conference committee was appointed by a vote of 65 yeas, 42 nays, and 75 not voting.

Davis and his committee hurried across the building to Wade and the Ohio Senator went back on the floor with faint hope that he could get his colleagues to rescind the amendment and enact the House bill. It took but a few moments. He got the floor, made the motion, and the Davis bill—now the Wade-Davis bill, passed by 18 to 14, with 17 senators absent. It was not a vote for a plan of reconstruction; it was, at best, merely a slap at Abraham Lincoln. The scant majorities, the absence of debate, and the number of absentees bore testimony to the apathy with which the lawmakers regarded both the subject and the President.

It was July 2. On Independence Day, as the session of Congress ground to a close, Abraham Lincoln went to the Capitol to sign bills as they came from the legislative hopper. Anxiously, a group of Radical senators, impatiently waiting, saw Lincoln push aside the Wade-Davis bill. Eager to press the issue—or to hide it—Michigan's Zachariah Chandler called the bill to the President's attention. If vetoed, it would hurt the party fearfully in the Northwest, Chandler said. "The important point is that one prohibiting slavery in the reconstructed states."

"That is a point on which I doubt the authority to act," replied the President.[19]

The Radicals, who had hoped that the growing evidence of failure for Lincoln's plan would lead him to surrender control of reconstruction to Congress, were indignant. Five days later they were outraged. In an unprecedented act Lincoln issued a proclamation giving his reasons for not signing the Wade-Davis bill. He was unprepared, he explained, to commit himself to one inflexible plan of reconstruction. He did not want to jeopardize the promising beginnings already made in Arkansas and Louisiana. If any state, however, wished to follow the procedures of the congressional plan, he would order the military authorities to coöperate.

Abraham Lincoln could not have expected his pocket veto and his proclamation to be accepted without protest. He was making a direct challenge to the Radical leaders of his party and forcing them to action. The leaders met the challenge. On August 5 Ben Wade and Winter Davis, consulting in a New York hotel room, met the unprecedented presidential proclamation with an unprecedented "manifesto." Indignant, they pointed out that Lincoln said nothing about Rebel leaders, nothing at all about the Rebel debt. It left slavery where it had been before the war. His proclamation was indeed a political "manifesto" against the friends of the government. But most of all the Radicals stressed the theme of usurpation. Lincoln, they said, was admittedly prepared to execute a policy which was not law—it was a "grave executive usurpation."

[19] *Ibid.*, XXXIV (1), 82 (Dec. 22, 1863); XXXIV (2), 1737-1740 (Apr. 19, 1864); XXXIV (3-4), 2096-2097, 2103-2108, 2117-3451 (May 4-July 1, 1864).

The first reaction, even of the Radicals, was one of shock. "Very bad taste," said the Chicago *Tribune*, and "hot-headed precipitancy." "Unjust and malignant attack on the president," thought the Wisconsin *State Journal*. And the New York *Times* turned upon the authors of the manifesto: "They have sanctioned the war not as a means of restoring the Union, but to free the slaves, seize the lands, crush the spirit, destroy the rights, and blot out forever the political freedom of the people inhabiting the Southern States." Considering the reaction, Lincoln might have remained content.[20] The final decision would depend on the outcome of the presidential election.

[20] Eben G. Scott, *Reconstruction During the Civil War* . . . (Boston, 1895), 298; New York *Tribune*, Aug. 5, New York *Times*, Aug. 9, Chicago *Tribune*, Aug. 11, *Wisconsin State Journal* (Madison), Aug. 12, 1864.

Chapter VI

The Uncompleted Contest

THE WADE-DAVIS "MANIFESTO" brought the issue into sharp focus, and for the remaining eight months of Abraham Lincoln's life, reconstruction was never far from the first place in his mind. Radical Republicans and critical Democrats alike saw in Lincoln's announced plan and developing program the clear specter of executive usurpation. The Democrats, however, were inclined to remain relatively quiet while Lincoln and the Radicals battled over the issue.

Back of each of the contending positions was an elaborate theory of the nature of the Union and of the war. Each of the protagonists bolstered his contentions and his actions with constitutional rationalization. In the Radical arsenal was the argument advanced by Charles Sumner that the Southern states had committed suicide. By their acts of secession they had ceased to exist as bodies politic, their laws were null and their property no longer protected by legal authority. Into this political vacuum Congress could move, establish law, and determine what kinds of property it would protect. It might also determine which inhabitants of the region might be admitted to political rights. Senator Sumner's theory of political and economic anarchy in the South was unrealistic and too drastic for a people whose nature abhorred a political vacuum. The Massachusetts Senator won few adherents. More appealing was the dogmatic assertion of Thaddeus Stevens, vindictive, acute, and realistic congressman from Pennsylvania. The Southern states, Stevens admitted, had seceded from the Union. They had established a government and had waged a war. The war was bringing victory to Northern arms, and the area of the Southern Confederacy was conquered territory—its lands, its people, and its political future were completely at the disposal of the victor.

Both Stevens and Sumner based their theories on the fact of secession, but Abraham Lincoln rested his case on the doctrine that the Union was perpetual. The Southern states had not seceded. Instead, evil men had seized the governments of the states and had used the apparatus of the state for evil purposes. But the states, the laws, and the property protected by those laws had not ceased to exist. As Lincoln would eventually express it, the states were out of their "proper practical relations" to the national government. The wicked men who had performed the evil act might be punished or forgiven by the President, but the states had not ceased to exist. The President's task was simple: restore them to their proper practical relations.

Bolstering each opposing constitutional argument was a moral appeal. Back of Lincoln's position lay the concepts of humanitarianism and forgiveness and Christian charity. Back of the Radicals were the appeals of human rights and social justice. Lincoln would forgive repentant sinners; the Radicals would wipe out a social evil and establish a greater democracy. In the vocabulary of controversy both antagonists had persuasive arguments, and neither made stark avowal of other objectives. The Democrats, however, could invoke a plague on both houses, accusing the Radicals of predatory designs on Southern property, and accusing Lincoln of ambition to be a dictator.

Yet, whatever the hidden motives of the contenders, there was a strange combination of logic and *non sequitur* in the position of each. No ardent Secessionist would be consistent in objecting to either Sumner's or Stevens' constitutional theories, and had Secessionists reacted on the basis of pure reason, those who had taken up arms against national centralization should have sought an alliance with Radical congressmen who were battling against executive dictatorship. And, had Lincoln sought absolute power, he might have found the enfranchised Negro a more pliable instrument of power than the discordant loyalists and the semipenitent Confederates whom he was trying to organize. Then, to compound the paradoxes, neither the theory of the perpetual union nor of the conquered provinces carried with it the necessary implication that reconstruction was the exclusive function of either the executive or the legislative branch of the government.

In any case, whatever the clarity of the opposing positions, the issue never came before the great tribunal of the American electorate. After the presidential election of 1864 Lincoln wanted to contend that his plans and proceedings had received a mandate from the people. But the voters had had no opportunity to choose between the two Republican positions. For a time it seemed indeed that they might have the issue clearly presented. After the Wade-Davis Manifesto, Davis—a malignant and ambitious man, said a Wisconsin paper—and a handful of anti-Lincoln Radicals met in convention and nominated John C. Frémont for the presidency on a completely Abolitionist-Radical platform. The Frémont candidacy brought confusion and concern in the Lincoln camp and threatened to take enough Republican votes from the regular nominees to throw the election to Democrat George B. McClellan. Yet, even the Radicals, who opposed Lincoln, recognized the necessity for a united front and deserted Frémont. The Union League clubs poured out Lincoln pamphlets and rallied to the President. Eventually, Lincoln made a bargain with Frémont's supporters and the Radical candidate reluctantly withdrew from the contest. The terms of the bargain had no direct connection with reconstruction and Frémont's withdrawal deprived Republican voters of the opportunity of deciding between conflicting views of reconstruction. The contest in 1864 was between Lincoln and McClellan, and, whereas peace proposals and the conduct of the war were in dispute, the processes of reconstruction were not directly at issue. Perhaps, if the Democrats had nominated their ablest man,

Horatio Seymour, the question of executive power and Lincoln's rotten boroughs in the South might have been debated on the hustings.

Although the election of 1864 gave no decision on the methods of reconstruction, it proved again Lincoln's power to control elections. The system of arbitrary arrests, military control of the polling places, and soldier voting, first applied in the Border States and then extended into the North, had saved the Republican party in 1862 and 1863. The election of 1864 saw a new extension of the system and demonstrated its continuing value in winning elections.

With a sure appreciation of political realities, Lincoln concluded that the election would be close. In August he was despondent. At a cabinet meeting he displayed an envelope containing a memorandum not to be opened until after the election. "This morning as for some days past," it read, "it seems exceedingly probable that this administration will not be elected. Then it will be my duty to so coöperate with the President-elect as to save the Union between the election and the inauguration; as he will have secured his election on such grounds that he cannot possibly save it afterwards." At the same time Henry J. Raymond, editor of the New York *Times* and the chairman of the national committee of the "Union" party, was writing Simon Cameron in Pennsylvania that "nothing but the most vigorous co-operation of all Union men can carry us through. I hear from every quarter the most discouraging accounts." Raymond proposed giving a fillip to the campaign by having Lincoln propose a peace conference to Jefferson Davis. This was, however, the low point in Republican morale. In September, with the adjustment of the Frémont aberration and with a successful new draft into the army going off without riot and disturbance, and with the Democrats showing no appreciable increase in the Maine and Vermont elections, prospects brightened. Then, in October came elections in Indiana and Pennsylvania, and it became evident that the system that had won in Ohio the year before was still useful.

In both the Hoosier and the Keystone states there had been troubles, and the administration leaders generally had been much concerned. In Pennsylvania, which might normally have been safely Republican, the Democrats made a vigorous campaign, stressing the draft, abolitionism, and centralization, while the Republicans were split into two contentious factions—one supporting Simon Cameron, Lincoln's first secretary of war, and the other backing Andrew Curtin, the bombastic governor running for re-election. In Indiana, Governor Oliver P. Morton, efficient and aggressive, was running for re-election. Morton's roughshod tactics with his political opponents produced a reaction but his energy and ingenuity were equal to the occasion. His adjutant-general harried Democrats during the campaign; an agent-provocateur enrolled Democrats in a secret society and then turned the names over to Morton; and on the eve of the election Morton flamboyantly arrested a handful of ratty conspirators, whom he charged with treason. He used the situation as an excuse for sending soldiers to the polls. Troops from Sherman's army came home for the election and the Nineteenth Vermont, passing through, stopped long enough to vote for Morton.[1]

On election night Lincoln, John Hay, his private secretary, and several others went over to the War Department to sit by the telegraph. A year before the President had sat there anxiously checking the returns from Ohio. This night the news produced no anxious moments. Pennsylvania seemed safe enough, and soldiers in the field and hospitals were voting properly. After an hour an enthusiastic report announced that Morton had a 30,000 vote lead. It was signed "McKin." "Who's that?" asked Lincoln. "A quartermaster of mine," answered Stanton. "He was sent there to announce that." In fact, added the Secretary of War, "a very healthy sentiment was growing up among the quartermasters."

[1] July 22, 1864 (Simon Cameron Papers, Library of Congress); Nicolay to Bates, Sept. 18 and Colfax to Lincoln, July 25, 1864 (JGNP).

A few days after the October elections Lincoln made a careful calculation of the best that the "Copperhead" ticket could receive. He counted in the Republican column the six New England states with 39 votes, gave New York, Pennsylvania, New Jersey, Delaware, and Maryland to McClellan; claimed Ohio, Indiana, Michigan, Wisconsin, Iowa, and Minnesota for Republicans; gave Missouri and Kentucky to the Democrats; took Oregon and California to himself; and claimed the new states of Kansas, West Virginia, and Nevada. Illinois he put in the Democratic column. The totals, which clearly gave every possible state to McClellan, were a narrow majority for the Republicans: 120 to 114. Clearly the picture was hopeful, but there was nothing in the prospect to warrant relaxing.[2]

Warned by the discussion of the Davis bill, Lincoln omitted the electoral votes of the Southern states. West Virginia he counted, but not Pierpont's "Restored" Virginia, nor Banks's government in Louisiana, or even Andrew Johnson's Tennessee. Although he did not count them in his estimate, he watched them carefully as they proceeded to go through the processes of choosing presidential electors.

In Louisiana, General Banks and newly-installed Governor Michael Hahn were proceeding with the work of reorganizing the state. Henry Winter Davis heard that only one-third of the state, with 233,000 of the state's population of 708,000, was inside the Union lines. Kentucky's Senator Lazrous Powell was watching, too. He agreed with the Radicals that the 6,000 votes cast for delegates to a constitutional convention were insufficient for a civil government and pointed out that Banks had confessed that the City of New Orleans was the State of Louisiana.[3] Even in Louisiana, when the convention met, one delegate struck

---

[2] Tyler Dennett (ed.), *Lincoln and the Civil War in the Diaries and Letters of John Hay* (New York, 1939), 228-229; Paul M. Angle (comp.), *New Letters and Papers of Abraham Lincoln* (New York, 1930), 362.
[3] *CG*, 38 Cong., 2 Sess., XXXV (2), 1069 (Feb. 24, 1865).

a discordant note by asserting that the convention could not sit three hours, if the military were withdrawn.

Yet, despite the doubts in both New Orleans and Washington, the convention re-made the constitution, and in Washington—just four days after the Wade-Davis Manifesto—Lincoln was encouraged. He wrote Banks that he was pleased with the constitution and was anxious that it be ratified. He would even give what help he could. "I will thank you," he wrote, "to let the civil officers in Louisiana, holding under me, know this is my wish and let me know at once who of them openly declares for the constitution and who of them, if any, declines so to declare." Throughout September the Union Leagues, Federal troops, civilian appointees of the President, and state officers staged mass meetings for the constitution, and at the same time passed resolutions endorsing the ticket of Lincoln and Johnson. On the eve of the election the military turned out all government and quartermaster employees for a torchlight procession in New Orleans. The next day 6,836 voters approved the constitution—although 1,570 hardy holdouts voted against it. The election was so conclusive that there was no point in repeating it in November. The legislature merely provided that it would select the electors to cast the state's seven electoral votes for the President. Four years before only South Carolina had selected electors by the legislature.[4]

The comparative peace of the campaign of 1864 in Louisiana had no parallel in Tennessee. There the process of state-making had been long delayed and, although Andrew Johnson had been military governor since April, 1862, he had not called for a state election or for a constitutional convention. Military activities in the state had of course been partly responsible, but a major factor in the delay had been the widening divisions between the Volunteer State's "loyal" Union men. Local elections for county offices had returned "Conservatives" in areas not strictly policed by soldiers. On the other hand, Union Leagues

[4] Caskey, 111-150.

had been active in organizing the electorate in Memphis and Nashville, and the Unionists of East Tennessee, once they were free of the Confederate occupation, had held meetings and passed resolutions. But the political activities had revealed that there were loyal men who did not accept the Emancipation Proclamation, did not favor an abolitionist war, and would not take Lincoln's oath of amnesty promising to accept all future presidential pronouncements on slavery. Opposed to the "Conservatives" were the "Unconditional Union" men who endorsed emancipation and abolition and looked forward to a complete reorganization of Tennessee's social and economic life.

Early in September the Unconditional Unionists called a convention at Nashville to discuss the condition of the country, the reorganization of civil government, and the expediency of holding a presidential election. At the moment when the delegates from East Tennessee, many of whom were Conservatives, were about to set out, a raid by Confederate cavalry under General Joseph Wheeler prevented their departure. The convention met, however, admitted all delegates who had been selected by regular conventions, and then threw the meeting open to all Unconditional Unionists. With the convention thus packed, a steering committee reported elaborately on all questions. There should be a convention of loyal people to revise the constitution. There should be a presidential election in November. The electors should be registered and all oath-taking citizens, all white men who had been soldiers in the Federal army and had been residents for six months, and all "known active friends of the government of the United States" should be allowed to vote. Further, the committee proposed that the polls should be open at the county seats, "guarded and protected so as to secure a fair and free election." Polls should also be opened for soldiers at their camps. A state militia, said the committee, should be immediately enrolled, organized, and armed. The convention adopted the report and Governor Johnson immediately announced that an election would be held under the convention's plan.[5]

The election machinery was definitely set to insure Republican victory. The Conservatives met, however, selected an electoral ticket pledged to McClellan, and sent a delegation to Washington to protest to Lincoln against Johnson's scheme. Specifically, they complained about having but one polling place in each county, about the imposition of oaths, about citizenship being based upon state rather than county residence, and about the proposed military interference. The protestors met short shrift from Abraham Lincoln. "May I inquire how long it took you and the New York politicians to concoct that paper?" he sneered. "Let General McClellan's friends manage their side of this contest in their own way and I will manage my side of it my way," he added.

Unfortunately for the Democrats, the election machinery was not in their hands to manage. Since, however, some of the protestors were among the leading Unionists of undoubted loyalty—Congressman T. A. R. Nelson, General William Campbell, and political leaders Bailey Peyton and Emerson Etheridge, for examples—Lincoln made a formal reply to their protest. He had had little time to reflect on the matter and their visit caught him unprepared, he began, as if half apologizing for his brusque manner. But he quickly reasserted his position. "My conclusion is that I have nothing to do with the matter. . . . By the constitution and the laws the President is charged with no duty in the conduct of a presidential election in any state." He could perceive no menace or coercion in Johnson's plan, and "leaving it alone will be your perfect security." Johnson would not molest Democrats—so long as they stayed away from the polls. Of course, Lincoln added, it would belong "to another department of the government" to decide if the votes of Tennessee were to be counted. With such an answer, the McClellan ticket withdrew from the contest. The people of Tennessee were, they announced, overawed by military

[5] *AP*, IV, 764.

power. The election in November chose electors for Lincoln and Johnson.[6]

As it turned out, the Republican ticket did not need the electoral votes of Tennessee, Arkansas, Louisiana, or Virginia. In the electoral college Lincoln received 212 votes while McClellan had but 21 from New Jersey, Kentucky, and Delaware, but without the aid of the military and the counting of soldier votes cast in the field, McClellan would have had a majority in the electoral college. In October, Lincoln had lumped the 39 votes of New England in the Republican column, and so it turned out. Connecticut's six votes were there only because the legislature had provided for gathering votes from soldiers in the field. The soldiers with "remarkable unanimity," as two patriotic historians put it shortly after the war, cast 2,898 votes, while Connecticut went for Lincoln by but 2,406. A combination of circumstances rescued New York's 33 votes which Lincoln had tentatively conceded to the "Copperheads." State commissioners carrying Democratic ballots to soldiers wound up in Old Capitol Prison in Washington, where they stayed until after election day. Other ballots were held in post offices and some sick soldiers getting home in time to vote found that Democratic ballots they had put in envelopes in the field had been removed and Republican tickets substituted. Steamers left City Point in Virginia filled with troops going home to vote, and even the provost-marshal of Grant's army complained that "all possible obstacles were thrown in the way of a fair soldier vote." On election eve General B. F. Butler arrived in New York to maintain order. There was no disorder. The Democratic vote declined and Horatio Seymour's supporters made substantial charges that the changes of votes, the suppression of soldier votes, and intimidation had carried the state for Lincoln.[7] And in Maryland, which Lincoln had conceded,

[6] *Ibid.*, IV, 766-777; Hall, 151.
[7] W. A. Crofutt and John M. Morris, *The Military and Civil History of Connecticut During the War of 1861-1865* (New York, 1869), 636; Marcelus R. Patrick Journal, Nov. 5, 1864 (Library of Congress);

the election was rescued by the adoption of a new state constitution. Late in October a new, Radical constitution went before the voters. By the existing laws and constitution, soldiers could not vote, but the new constitution permitted voting in the field. The civilian population turned down the new document by a majority of 375, but soldiers voting under the new document overturned the civilian majority. One week after the new constitution, which disfranchised Rebel sympathizers, went into effect, came the presidential election. The day before the election General Lew Wallace entered Baltimore with troops to patrol the polls and to enforce the disfranchising provisions of the new constitution. The vote of Baltimore dropped from 30,155 in 1860 to 17,610—and of that, McClellan garnered 2,776. Lincoln's majority of 12,000 in Baltimore was enough to overcome McClellan's lead of 7,000 in the rest of the state.[8]

It was, in many places, as much the count as it was the casting of the soldier vote. In 1941, seventy-seven years after the election of 1864, packages of Ohio soldier votes, cast by units in the field and duly forwarded to the Secretary of State, were opened for the first time under the supervision of the Ohio State Archeological and Historical Society. The sealed packages bore on the outside the figures of the Lincoln and McClellan votes that each contained, but the penciled notations bore no ascertainable relation to the contents. The ballots were threaded together through their centers and in most cases the threaded needle rested in a rusty groove on the top ballot. The vote was overwhelmingly for Lincoln, but the ballots themselves bore testimony to the difficulty confronting the soldier who wished to defy his fellows and his officers by casting a vote for McClellan. Republican soldiers had regular ballots, printed by the Republican party and distributed to the troops. Few official Democratic ballots were in the packages. Some of McClellan's supporters had clipped sample ballots from news-

ORA, 3, IV, 873; David G. Croly, Seymour and Blair (New York, 1868), 128-131ff.
    [8] William L. Seabrook, Maryland's Great Part in Saving the Union . . . (Westminster, 1913), 54-56.

papers and many had laboriously copied the electoral ticket
in their own handwriting on scraps of papers. In the
packages were the rejected ballots, thrown out by officers
acting as election officials in the camps. Without exception,
the rejected ballots were Democratic: irregularities in the
spelling of Cincinnati, Coshocton, or Chillicothe from where
a Democratic elector came was sufficient to invalidate a
ballot. Yet, the work of the election officials in the camps
was a work of supererogation: the official returns on the
units in the field bore no resemblance to the vote as cast.
Actually, the Secretary of State gave McClellan a better
vote than he got in the field, but in no case enough to call
Lincoln's overwhelming victory into question.

Without the soldier vote and the discouragement of Democrats at the polls, the electoral vote might have stood 122
for McClellan and 112 for Lincoln. Even so, however,
Lincoln would have had a majority of the popular vote—a
reversal of the situation four years before. Perhaps, indeed, had McClellan carried the electoral college without
having a popular majority, the congressional Radicals
might not have scorned Lincoln's "rotten boroughs" in the
Southern states.

Yet, the situation in two of the states that McClellan
carried might have given pause to the politicians. In both
Kentucky and Delaware McClellan won. These were states
where military intervention had brought earlier Republican
successes. In 1862 Kentucky had been saved by arresting
Democrats and patrolling the polls, but the momentary
quieting of the state had resulted in its slipping into the
opposition. In Delaware's special congressional election on
November 19, 1863 General Robert Schenck's soldiers had
insured the election of Congressman William Cannon. On
October 27, 1864 Cannon wrote in alarm to Secretary
Stanton that troops would be needed at the polls to keep
the peace and prevent riot and bloodshed. He asked for
the return of Delaware men in the Veterans Reserve Corps,
and furloughs for three regiments of infantry near Peters-
burg and the Delaware cavalry guarding the Baltimore and

Ohio Railroad. "Without the vote of our troops in the field it will be utterly impossible to carry our state, and the election of U. S. Senator, representatives to Congress, and Emancipation in Delaware depend upon the result."[9] But Stanton was negligent, and Lincoln was not concerned with Delaware's three votes. McClellan carried the state by a majority of 612, and a Democrat went to Congress. The lesson, which no practical politician could overlook, was clear. The system of soldier voting and military intervention at the polls would be worthless, when the war was over. In another presidential election the votes of the Southern states would be needed.

The lessons of the election seemed to stiffen the determination of both Charles Sumner and Abraham Lincoln. To a large extent the issue became personal. "Questions of statesmanship press for decision," Sumner told the Englishman John Bright on New Year's Day, 1865. "The President is exerting every force to bring Congress to receive Louisiana under the Banks government. I do not believe that Louisiana is strong enough in loyalty and freedom for an independent state . . . . I have discussed it with the President and have tried to impress on him the necessity of having no break between him and Congress." And Lincoln was equally disgusted with the Senator. "I can do nothing with Mr. Sumner in these matters," he said in exasperation. "While Mr. Sumner is very cordial with me, he is making his history in an issue with me on this very point."

Making his history though he was, Sumner was willing to concede a little. Privately, he proposed that he would let Louisiana be recognized, if Lincoln would demand Negro suffrage in all the other Rebel states. But the President was adamant. He believed that he had a majority of the Congress behind him. He asquiesced when Congress formally rejected the electoral votes of the Southern states, and he said nothing, when Sumner denounced the Pierpont government of Virginia as nothing more than the common

[9] Edwin M. Stanton Papers (Library of Congress).

council of Alexandria. General Banks and two newly-elected senators from Louisiana were present in Washington lobbying for admission. Lincoln might well have felt confident in refusing to accept Negro suffrage.

He reckoned, however, without considering Sumner's persistence and his determination to "make his history" on the issue of civil rights and Negro suffrage. Sumner realized that one argument of the President's supporters would be that Louisiana and the other reconstructing states would be needed to ratify the Thirteenth Amendment. On February 11 he attempted to forestall that argument with resolutions contending that, since the Southern states had committed suicide, only three-fourths of the loyal states were needed to adopt the amendment. Further, Sumner proposed that the representation of any state be determined, not by population, but by the number of male voters—a device he hoped would bribe the Southerners to admit Negroes to the polls. But the proposals met no favor. As the New York *Times* pointed out, February 6, 10, 1865, changing the base of representation would cost Massachusetts one House seat and one electoral vote. The paper denounced Sumner's "excessive zeal" for the black men: his plan was "wrong in principle" and "pernicious in effect."[10]

Encouraged by Sumner's lack of support, Illinois Senator Lyman Trumbull brought in a resolution to recognize Louisiana, and on February 25 moved its discussion. Tactically, the resolution was unwise, for Sumner immediately began a filibuster that threatened to hold up all legislation. To his aid came Ben Wade and other extreme Radicals and even Democrat Powell. The Kentuckian denied that a major-general had a right to go into any state to dictate who could vote, and that Congress had a right to ratify the Louisiana constitution. The discussion made no contribution to the controversy. It gave Wade a chance to repeat that Lincoln's scheme was "monarchical," and John B. Henderson of Missouri the chance to ask, "Mr. President, do you

[10] Nicolay and Hay, X, 85; Boston *Daily Advertiser*, Jan. 7, 1871; Boston *Commonwealth*, March 11, 1865.

suppose you will ever have loyalty in the Southern States if you undertake to govern them by generals and provost marshals for all time to come?" It brought from Sumner the unequivocal declaration that the Republicans needed the Negroes' ballots as much as they once needed their bullets. As for the Louisiana government, he pronounced it, in true Sumnerian invective, as "a mere seven months' abortion, begotten by the bayonet, in criminal conjunction with the spirit of caste, and born before it's time, rickety, unformed, unfinished, whose continued existence will be a burden, a reproach, and a wrong."

In the midst of the filibuster there came an interchange, enlivening the dull pages of the *Congressional Globe,* which threw light on Sumner's mental processes. He had been interrupted by Senator Reverdy Johnson of Maryland. Turning on him, Sumner asked, "The Senator then thinks that Ohio can enslave a fellow man?" "Just as much as Massachusetts can," asnwered Johnson. "Massachusetts cannot," asserted Sumner. "Why not?" asked Johnson. "Massachusetts cannot do an act of injustice," declared Sumner, while his fellows laughed.

The filibuster had its effect. In order to get the ordinary business of Congress completed before the session ended, Lincoln's men withdrew the Louisiana resolution, and the President stood defeated. Democrats joined with moderate Republicans in denouncing Sumner's "outrageous parliamentary tactics" and "factious opposition." As Lincoln saw it, the Radicals who insisted on Negro suffrage were attempting "to change this government from its original form and make it a strong centralized power." But Sumner explained his purpose in a broader frame of reference than a mere political and constitutional one. "Can emancipation be carried out," he asked John Bright, "without using the lands of the slave masters? We must see that the freemen are established on the soil. The great plantations must be broken up and the freedmen must have the pieces." Then, unless the Negroes were given the franchise, "the old enemy will reappear" and "in alliance with the northern democracy, put us all in peril again, postpone the day of tranquillity and menace the national credit by assailing the national debt." In Sumner's mind, social reform and economic reorganization depended on the Negroes controlling the Southern states. "It is said they are as intelligent as the Irish just arrived," he added. "Mr. Lincoln," he sighed, "is slow in accepting truths."[11]

Lincoln was indeed slow in accepting Sumner's formulation of truth. Yet, as a pragmatist, he was forced to recognize that each of his plans of reconstruction—the patronage, the governments-in-exile, the military governors, the efforts to organize the Southern Unionists, and the offer of amnesty to a repentant 10 per cent of the Confederates—all had met failure. He had no fanatic devotion to principles drawn from the empyrean, like Senator Sumner; no predatory designs on the property of Southerners like many Radicals; yet, he was unwilling to give up the struggle in the face of repeated failure.

There was, under the circumstances, one course left, if the nation was to be re-made with a minimum of social economic, and political revolution—an appeal to Northerners and Southerners alike for magnanimity, for repentance and forgiveness. "Let us strive on," he pleaded in his second inaugural a few days after Sumner's filibuster ended,". . . to bind up the nation's wounds, to secure a just and lasting peace among ourselves and with all nations." It was, perhaps, the most practical appeal he could make. The American people were a Christian people, committed in theory to the practice of charity, to the dogma of the forgiveness of sins. The Parable of the Prodigal Son was a part of the American ethic.

In the five remaining weeks of his life Abraham Lincoln began to formulate yet a new plan of reconstruction. The war was coming to a close and on March 27 Lincoln went to City Point to discuss with General Grant the plans for

[11] Pierce, *Memoirs and Letters of Charles Sumner*, I, 219, 221-226; *CG*, 38 Cong., 2 Sess., XXXV (2), 1060-1070, 1097, 1126-1129 (Feb. 24-27, 1865) ; New York *World*, Feb. 28, New York *Herald*, March 1, 1865.

the end. To the meeting came General Sherman and Admiral David Porter. With them Lincoln talked about the disposition of the Rebel states. He wanted, he said, to get peace quickly, and the deluded Rebel soldiers back to their homes. He contemplated no harsh measures, no revenge. He implied—with a typical story to illustrate the point—that he would be pleased, if Jefferson Davis could escape the country "unbeknownst to me." He implied that Sherman should get the surrender of General Joseph E. Johnston's army on whatever terms possible, and that Sherman should tell North Carolina's Governor Z. B. Vance that, as soon as the Rebel armies laid down their arms, the citizens would be protected in their civil pursuits. Moreover, as Sherman remembered it, Lincoln authorized him to tell Vance that, in order to avoid anarchy, the "state government then in existence" would be recognized as a *de facto* government until Congress might act.[12] Unfortunately, when Sherman met Johnston and embodied his understandings in a convention which amounted to a treaty of peace, Lincoln was dead and the Radical spirit of revenge ruled the cabinet. But before the press, a congressional committee and the public, Sherman maintained that Lincoln's counsels were those of conciliation and forgiveness.

That Sherman correctly understood Lincoln became evident a week after the meeting at City Point. Hardly had Lincoln got back to Washington than Richmond fell. Lincoln hurried off to the Rebel capital. There he talked to leading Virginians, among them former Supreme Justice John A. Campbell, who far back in the days of the Sumter crisis, tried to avoid a conflict. Now Judge Campbell hoped to arrange an armistice and negotiate a peace. Lincoln's terms were the simple recognition of the national authority, the acceptance of emancipation, and the discharge of the Rebel armies. Campbell agreed and began to discuss details for implementing the plan. There was the question of Pierpont's government at Alexandria, and there was also a proposal to reassemble the Confederate legislature of

[12] *Memoirs*, II, 324-331.

Virginia for the purpose of withdrawing Virginia troops in
Lee's army.   To Major-General Godfrey Weitzel, provost
marshal of Richmond, Lincoln issued an order to permit "the
gentlemen who have acted as the Legislature of Virginia" to
reassemble to "take measures to withdraw the Virginia
troops and other support from resistance to the General
Government."   Should they reassemble, Lincoln ordered,
"Give them permission and protection until, if at all, they
attempt some action hostile to the United States."

About the meaning of this order and about Lincoln's
intentions controversy arose immediately.   Campbell assumed that the legislature could act on all matters looking
to ending "resistance to the General Government" and could
stay in session until it attempted hostile action.   Probably,
Campbell understood rightly, for Lincoln went back to
Washington to discuss the arrangements with his cabinet.
He was astonished at the disapproval he met.   Secretary of
War Stanton and Attorney General Joseph Speed were
vehement.[13]   To Gideon Welles, who was not quite so out-
spoken, the President attempted an explanation.   The Virginia legislature was composed of the prominent and in-
fluential men of the counties and he wished them to "come
together and turn themselves and their neighbors into good
Union men."   There must be, said Lincoln, courts, and law
and order, or society would be broken up, the disbanded
armies turned into robber bands or guerillas.   But Welles
was not convinced.   He too raised the question of Pierpont's
government.

Defeated by the lack of support in his own cabinet, Lincoln yielded once more, and for the last time, on a tentative
plan of reconstruction.   At Stanton's insistence he sent a
telegram to Weitzel.   Since Lee's armies had now surrendered, there was no reason to reassemble the legislature.
Judge Campbell, he explained, had assumed that "I have
called the insurgent Legislature of Virginia together, as

[13] Henry G. Connor, *John Archibald Campbell* . . .   (Boston, 1920),
182-183; Raoul S. Narroll, "Lincoln and the Sherman Peace Fiasco—
Another Fable?" *Journal of Southern History*, XX, 459-483 (Nov.,
1954).

the rightful Legislature of the State, to settle all differences with the United States. I have done no such thing."

Instead, Lincoln pointed out, he had called them "the gentlemen who have acted as the Legislature" and he had authorized their meeting only to withdraw Virginia's troops from Lee. This, of course, was technically true, but it was much less than the plan Lincoln had presented to the cabinet and argued for with Welles. Campbell, who had discussed the matter with him, thought the President had resorted to a technicality to quibble out of an agreement.[14]

The collapse of this, Lincoln's last plan of reconstruction, left the President without a program. Defeated in succession by the quarrels among Unionists he had hoped to unite, by the failure of Confederates to respond to offers of amnesty, by Radical insistence on programs that contemplated social reform and economic penetration of the South, and even by the revolt of his cabinet, Lincoln made his last public pronouncement on reconstruction with only an attitude to recommend to the victorious Northern people. Returned from Richmond, Lincoln spoke from the White House portico to celebrants who assembled to serenade him. Victory, said the President, made reconstruction press more closely. "It is fraught with great difficulty." It was, he explained, not like a foreign war in which an "authorized organ" might negotiate a peace. "We must begin with a mold from disorganized and discordant elements." The situation was worse because "we, the loyal people, differ among ourselves as to the mode, manner, and means of reconstruction."

To resolve the difficulty the President—with true pragmatic approach—proposed ignoring the theories of the status of the Southern states. "We all agree that the seceded states are out of their proper practical relation with the

[14] Gideon Welles, *The Diary of the Secretary of the Navy Under Lincoln and Johnson* (Boston, 1909), III, 279-281; Randall and Current, 353-359; William M. Robinson, Jr., *Justice in Gray* . . . (Cambridge, 1941), 591-593; Ambler, 253-257.

Union." The only object of the government was to restore their proper practical relations.

He reviewed the case of Louisiana and his approach was, as it had been from the beginning, a political one. He would have preferred to enfranchise very intelligent Negroes and colored soldiers—but it was beside the point to complain that the Louisiana constitution was not all that might be desired. He would take and improve it rather than dishearten the loyal element. Then, once again, he struck the note that no inflexible plan should be prescribed. He was, he added, considering "some new announcement to the people of the South."[15]

The new plan never came. On the last day of his life Abraham Lincoln discussed reconstruction again with his cabinet, but no new plan came from the meeting. Three weeks later Andrew Johnson announced his plan of reconstruction and in the controversy that followed he alleged that he was carrying out Lincoln's plan. But Johnson's plan bore more resemblance to Henry Winter Davis' bill than to Lincoln's schemes. Perhaps, indeed, Lincoln might have come to that point, but Johnson's inflexible adherence to his own program was far removed from Lincoln's experimental, pragmatic approach to the problem. It is more likely that John Wilkes Booth's bullet found Abraham Lincoln without a plan of reconstruction.

Charles Sumner gave his attention to Lincoln's informal remarks on the White House portico. "The President's speech and other things," he remarked, "augur confusion and uncertainty in the future with hot controversy. Alas! Alas!"

It was indeed "Alas!" From the hot controversy that followed there grew the myth of Lincoln's Plan of Reconstruction as a plan which, had he but lived, would have healed the nation's wounds with love and forgiveness. Not a week had passed before the editor of a religious paper, who had been a consistent opponent of the war, struck the

[15] Basler, VIII, 400-405.

new note. "To the general interests of the people, South
and North, the prolonged life of Abraham Lincoln has
assumed, within the fortnight before his assassination, a
value it had lacked up to that period." Grant, said the
editor, had treated Lee with magnimity, "and since President Lincoln had shown the disposition to sustain General
Grant, in offering the Confederates terms they could accept
without utter degredation, there was a disposition growing
among wise and honest men to stand by him and support
him."[16] This early formulation of the myth found many
an elaboration while the "hot controversy" raged, and long
after the Radical plans for remoulding and reconstructing
the South, tried for a dozen years, proved as great failures
as Lincoln's war-time efforts, the belief grew strong that
Lincoln would have brought a different result. In the shock
of Lincoln's death men remembered only his last words and
forgot that for one or another reason, each of his plans
of reconstruction had failed.

Yet, if he had failed to effect a plan of reconstruction for
the South, Lincoln had still reconstructed the nation. In
the beginning he had rejected the compromise which would
have fastened a political dualism upon the United States.
Taking advantage of the exigencies of the war and the
necessities of politics, he had destroyed the rights and
powers of the states and had concentrated power in the
hands of the national government. At no time had he proposed to bring the Southern states back into the old Federal
Union. Instead, each of his plans, his programs, and his
processes had looked toward making the seceded states into
subordinate parts of a sovereign and centralized nation.
Perhaps, indeed, the war which the national government
had successfully waged against the states prevented the
restoration of the old Union and made imperative the
attempt to remodel Southern life in conformity with the
national model.

[16] Pierce, *Memoirs and Letters of Charles Sumner*, I, 238; *New York
Freeman's Journal and Catholic Register*, XVI, 4 (Apr. 22, 1865).

Bibliography

Manuscripts

Andrew Johnson Papers, John C. Crittenden Papers, Robert Todd Lincoln Papers, John C. Nicolay Papers, Simon Cameron Papers, Edwin M. Stanton Papers, Joseph Holt Papers, and the Marcellus R. Patrick Papers, Library of Congress, Washington, D. C.; Edward A. Atkinson Papers, Massachusetts Historical Society Library, Boston; William Francis Allen Diaries, Wisconsin State Historical Society Library, Madison; Richard Yates Papers, Illinois State Historical Library, Springfield; Isham G. Harris Collection, Tennessee State Historical Society, Nashville; B. F. Buckner Letters, University of Kentucky, Lexington.

Minutes of the Board of Directors of the Union League of Philadelphia, 1863; Minutes of the Meeting of the Union League Club of Boston, Feb.-March, 1863; and Union League of America of Illinois, Record Book of the Grand State Secretary, George H. Harlow, 1862-1865. These manuscripts are held by the Union League offices in Philadelphia, Boston, and Chicago, respectively. A microfilm copy of the last-named is in the Wisconsin State Historical Society, Madison.

Born, Katherine. "The Unionist Movement in East Tennessee During the Civil War and Reconstruction Period." Unpublished M. A. thesis, University of Wisconsin, 1933.

Silvestro, Clement M. "None but Patriots: The Union Leagues in Civil War and Reconstruction." Unpublished Ph.D. thesis, University of Wisconsin, 1959.

Books and Articles

Ambler, Charles H. *Francis H. Pierpont, Union War Governor of Virginia and Father of West Virginia.* Chapel Hill, 1937.

Angle, Paul M., comp. *New Letters and Papers of Abraham Lincoln.* New York, 1930.

Annual Message of the Governor of the State of New York, January 5, 1864. Albany, 1864.

Appleton's American Annual Cyclopaedia and Register of Important Events of the Years 1861-65. New York, 1864-1870.

Basler, Roy P., ed. *Collected Works of Abraham Lincoln.* New Brunswick, N. J., 1953. 8 vols.

Bellows, Henry W. *Historical Sketch of the Union League Club of New York.* New York, 1879.

Bentley, George R. *A History of the Freemen's Bureau.* Philadelphia, 1955.

Carman, Harry J. and Reinhard H. Luthin. *Lincoln and the Patronage.* New York, 1943.

Caskey, Willie M. *Secession and Restoration in Louisiana.* Baton Rouge, 1938.

Connor, Henry G. *John Archibald Campbell: Associate Justice of the United States Supreme Court, 1853-1861.* Boston, 1920.

Conrad, Henry S. *History of the State of Delaware.* Washington, 1908.

Coulter, E. Merton. *Civil War and Readjustment in Kentucky.* Chapel Hill, 1926.

Craven, Avery O. *The Growth of Southern Nationalism, 1848-1861.* Baton Rouge, 1953.

Crofutt, W. A. and John M. Morris. *The Military and Civil History of Connecticut During the War of 1861-1865.* New York, 1869.

Croly, David G. *Seymour and Blair*. New York, 1868.

Current, Richard N. *Old Thad Stevens*. Madison, 1942.

Dennett, Tyler, ed. *Lincoln and the Civil War in the Diaries and Letters of John Hay*. New York, 1939.

Grand Mass Meeting of Loyal Citizens . . . March 6, 1863. New York, 1863.

Hall, Clifton R. *Andrew Johnson, Military Governor of Tennessee*. Princeton, 1916.

Harper, Robert S. *Lincoln and the Press*. New York, 1951.

Hesseltine, William B. *Lincoln and the War Governors*. New York, 1955.

————. *Lincoln's Problems in Wisconsin*. Madison, 1952.

————. *The South in American History*. New York, 1943.

Holmes, Oliver W. *Oration Delivered . . . Boston*. Philadelphia, 1863.

Laws of the State of Mississippi . . . 1860. Jackson, 1860.

Lewis, Virgil A. *How West Virginia Was Made*. Charleston, W. Va., 1909.

Lieber, Francis. *Slave Plantations and the Yeomanry*. New York, 1863.

McCarthy, Charles H. *Lincoln's Plan of Reconstruction*. New York, 1901.

Mitgang, Herbert, ed. Noah Brooks, *Washington in Lincoln's Time*. New York, 1958.

Moore, Frank, ed. *The Rebellion Record, A Diary of American Events*. New York, 1864-1867. 10 vols.

Narroll, Raoul S. "Lincoln and the Sherman Peace Fiasco— Another Fable?" *Journal of Southern History*, XX, 459-483 (Nov., 1954).

New England Loyal Publication Society Papers, No. 90. Boston, 1865?

Nevins, Allan. *The Emergence of Lincoln.* New York, 1952. 2 vols.

Nicolay, John G. and John Hay. *Complete Works of Abraham Lincoln.* New York, 1905. 12 vols.

Parks, Joseph H. "John Bell and Secession," *East Tennessee Historical Society Publications,* XVI, 30-47 (1944).

Parton, James. *General Butler in New Orleans.* New York, 1864.

Pearson, Elizabeth W., ed. *Letters from Port Royal Written at the Time of the Civil War.* Boston, 1906.

Pierce, Edward L. *Memoirs and Letters of Charles Sumner.* Boston, 1894. 4 vols.

————. *The Negroes at Port Royal. Report of E. L. Pierce, Government Agent to the Hon. Salmon P. Chase, Secretary of the Treasury.* Boston, 1862.

Proceedings of the Grand Council of the Union League of America for the State of Illinois at Its Second Annual Session, September 2, 1863. Springfield, 1863.

Proceedings of the National Convention, Union League of America, Held at Cleveland, May 20 and 21, 1863. Washington, 1863.

Queener, Vernon M. "The Origin of the Republican Party in East Tennessee," *East Tennessee Historical Publications,* XX, 59-83 (1948).

Randall, James G. *The Civil War and Reconstruction.* Boston, 1953.

———— and Richard N. Current. *Lincoln the President: The Last Full Measure.* New York, 1958.

Reader, Frank S. *History of the Fifth West Virginia Cavalry.* New Brighton, Pa., 1890.

Report of the Executive Committee of the Grand National Council of the Union League of America, Dec. 14, 1864. Washington, 1864.

The Return of the Rebellious States to the Union, A Letter from Hon. William Whiting to the Union League of Philadelphia. Philadelphia, 1864.

Robinson, William M., Jr. *Justice in Gray: A History of the Judical System of the Confederate States of America.* Cambridge, 1941.

Scheips, Paul J. "Lincoln and the Chiriqui Colonization Project," *Journal of Negro History*, XXXVII, 418-453 (Oct., 1952).

Scott, Eben G. *Reconstruction During the Civil War in the United States of America.* Boston, 1895.

Seabrook, William L. *Maryland's Great Part in Saving the Union.* Westminster, 1913.

Shepard, Odell, ed. *The Journal of Amos Bronson Alcott.* Boston, 1938.

[Sherman, William T.] *Memoirs of General William Tecumseh Sherman.* New York, 1891. 2 vols.

Smith, Edward C. *The Borderland and the Civil War.* New York, 1927.

Smith, George W. "Broadsides for Freedom: Civil War Propaganda in New England," *New England Quarterly*, XXI, 291-312 (Sept., 1948).

Trefousse, Hans L. *Ben Butler, The South Called Him Beast!* New York, 1957.

War of the Rebellion: A Compilation of the Official Records of the Union and Confederate Armies. Washington, 1880-1901. 130 vols.

Welles, Gideon. *The Diary of the Secretary of the Navy Under Lincoln and Johnson.* Boston, 1909. 3 vols.

Wesley, Charles. "Lincoln's Plans for Colonizing the Emancipated Negroes," *Journal of Negro History*, IV, 7-21 (Jan., 1919).

Williams, T. Harry. *Lincoln and the Radicals.* Madison, 1941.

Wilson, James G. "General Halleck, A Memoir," *Journal of the Military Service Institutions of the United States,* XXXVI, 533-555 (1905).

Zorn, Roman J. "Minnesota Public Opinion and the Secession Controversy, December, 1860-April, 1861," *Mississippi Valley Historical Review,* XXXVI, 435-456 (Dec., 1949).

Magazines and Newspapers

Boston *Commonwealth,* 1865; Boston *Daily Advertiser,* 1863; Chicago *Tribune,* 1864; *Congressional Globe* (Washington), 1863-1865; *Demorest's New York Illustrated News,* 1862; Detroit *Free Press,* 1863; *Missouri Democrat* (St. Louis), 1864; New York *Evening Post,* 1863; *Freeman's Journal and Catholic Register* (New York), 1865; New York *Herald,* 1865; New York *Times,* 1861-1864; New York *Tribune,* 1863-1864; New York *World,* 1863-1865; *Wisconsin State Journal* (Madison), 1864.

Index